Chinese Music

Unique and complex in style, traditional Chinese music forms a fascinating part of China's cultural heritage. This accessible, illustrated introduction to Chinese music takes the reader through the 8,000-year history of China's musical instruments, the diversity of Chinese folk music, the development of China's famous operas, and the modern Chinese music industry. From classical to contemporary styles, Jin Jie explores the influence that Chinese music has had around the world.

Introductions to Chinese Culture

The thirty volumes in the Introductions to Chinese Culture series provide accessible overviews of particular aspects of Chinese culture written by a noted expert in the field concerned. The topics covered range from architecture to archaeology, from mythology and music to martial arts. Each volume is lavishly illustrated in full color and will appeal to students requiring an introductory survey of the subject, as well as to more general readers.

Jin Jie

CHINESE MUSIC

CAMBRIDGE
UNIVERSITY PRESS

CAMBRIDGE UNIVERSITY PRESS
Cambridge, New York, Melbourne, Madrid, Cape Town, Singapore,
São Paulo, Delhi, Dubai, Tokyo, Mexico City

Cambridge University Press
The Edinburgh Building, Cambridge CB2 8RU, UK

Published in the United States of America by Cambridge University Press,
New York

www.cambridge.org
Information on this title: www.cambridge.org/9780521186919

Originally published by China Intercontinental Press as
Chinese Music (9787508513294) in 2010

© China Intercontinental Press 2010

This updated edition is published by Cambridge University Press
with the permission of China Intercontinental Press under
the China Book International programme 🔵.

For more information on the China Book International programme, please visit
http://www.cbi.gov.cn/wisework/content/10005.html

Cambridge University Press retains copyright in its own contributions
to this updated edition

© Cambridge University Press 2011

First published 2011

A catalogue record for this publication is available from the British Library

ISBN 978-0-521-18691-9 Paperback

Contents

Preface

Music reflects people's thoughts and their sense of beauty and art, representing different cultures around the world. Chinese music is unique in style. Chinese musical instruments, of which there are many different varieties, constitute an important part of folk music, which, together with Chinese operas, have played an important part in the development of culture in China.

Chinese music has a long history. From the "twelve Lüs," with a history of more than 4,000 years, to the bone flute found in Henan dating to the Neolithic Age more than 8,000 years ago, a large variety of musical relics have been discovered, reflecting the skill of the ancient Chinese people.

During the Spring and Autumn and the Warring States periods (770–221 BC), music developed quickly. At that time, many types of musical instruments were created and improved, and the *Bayin* (eight tones) classification method was adopted.

During the Tang Dynasty (618–907), the state began to establish music management and education organizations. By the Song Dynasty (960–1279), Chinese opera had matured, while during the Yuan Dynasty (1279–1368), the styles of the south and north dramas were formed and many classics were created, including *The Injustice to Dou E* and *The Romance of the Western Chamber*. Since this time, Chinese music has been used to express human emotions.

In the Ming and Qing dynasties (1368–1911), music became more popular among ordinary people, and a variety of different kinds of operas developed. After the Sino-British Opium War in the mid-nineteenth century, traditional Chinese music and Western music sourced from Europe were integrated.

Since China's reform in 1978, music performance, education, musicology, and related publications and marketing have developed at a rapid pace.

The exchanges and conflicts that have taken place between Chinese and Western culture can be extended to the music world. The earliest musical exchanges recorded can be traced back more than 4,000 years. After Zhang Qian's diplomatic mission to Xiyu (the Western Regions in China) in the Western Han Dynasty, the musical instruments, song and dance of Central Asia and West Asia were introduced to the Central Plain through the "silk road," which made music more colorful. In the early twentieth century, western music was formally introduced into China. More and more people accepted western musical instruments and used them to perform and make music. Later in the century, Chinese musical instruments developed further after experiencing a period of isolation. Entering the twenty-first century, Chinese pop music has developed, while Chinese "new music" has undergone internationalized and integrated development through exchanges with western music.

Music is a symbol of the culture of a country. Its content, forms and styles are closely connected with the geographic, historical, linguistic and cultural conditions of a country, a region or a nation. Chinese music, after thousands of years of accumulation, has developed a rich pattern of plentiful styles, as well as embracing the coexistence of traditional and modern music.

Chapter 1
The Evolution of Chinese Music

Music is among the most significant achievements of human civilization, and Chinese music has played a part in this achievement. The number of Chinese folk songs collected so far totals more than 300,000 separate pieces. China also has more than 200 musical instruments and a huge variety of different musical genres. Chinese *quyi* and opera are both important musical genres, with the former divided into more than 200 categories and the latter into more than 360 categories. As this book will show, Chinese music has grown by absorbing and incorporating the disparate musical cultures of many different ethnic groups and regions over centuries and millennia.

Historically, music, both in China and abroad, appeared earlier than Chinese characters. Ancient Chinese literature typically attributed the origin of Chinese music to Emperor Huangdi, who lived more than 4,000 years ago. It is said that Emperor Huangdi once asked a necromancer named Lun to develop a regular sound system based on high and low-pitched sounds. This system was later called *Lü*. According to this legend, Lun found bamboo pipes in faraway places and listened carefully to the singing of male and female phoenixes, the divine birds of the ancient Chinese. He then made the bamboo pipes into twelve *Lü* pipes and called them the "twelve *Lü*s."

Recent archaeological discoveries show that the origins of music are even older than the legend of Lun suggests. A batch of bone flutes were unearthed in 1986–87 from a site dating to the Neolithic Age located in Jiahu Village, Wuyang County, Henan Province. Over 8,000 years old, these bone flutes are evidence of a highly developed musical culture in prehistoric China. Further evidence of this early musical culture came with the discovery of clay *xuns* (a type of ancient musical instrument) at the Hemudu Site in Zhejiang and Banpo Site in Xi'an, which are thought to be 6,000 years old.

Ancient Times

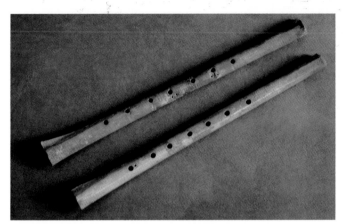

Bone flutes unearthed from the remains of the Neolithic Age at Jiahu Village, Henan Province between 1986 and 1987, are the most ancient musical instruments discovered by archeologists in China.

All music in early human history began with singing. As is written in the second-century BC text, *Huainanzi*: "Among the workers who carry lumber together, those walking in the front of the queue would shout '*yexu*,' which was echoed by those following them. This was the song for encouragement in carrying loads." This scene of workers chanting in unison while carrying a huge piece of wood together shows how we can trace the origins of primitive songs to daily labor. Lu Xun, a modern Chinese historian, argues that these labor chants (*haozi*) are in fact the earliest forms of Chinese poetry.

In the early history of civilization (around 2600–2100 BC), the arts of music and dancing did not exist as separate art forms with independent meaning. Music and dance were considered to be an integral part of religious ceremonies, particularly those relating to witchcraft. As such, music in this period is often shrouded in mystery and is referred to as "primitive music dance" because it features the integration of songs, dances and music. As Mao's preface to the *Book of Songs* states, "People used words to express their inner feelings, which were beyond words. Therefore they exclaimed but still failed to express themselves completely. They then turned to singing. When this was still inadequate, people unwittingly moved their hands and legs and danced." This description shows vividly the origin of dance as well as the relationships that existed between poems, songs, dances and music.

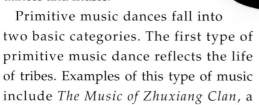

Primitive music dances fall into two basic categories. The first type of primitive music dance reflects the life of tribes. Examples of this type of music include *The Music of Zhuxiang Clan*, a

A pottery basin painted with dancing figures unearthed in 1973 at Shangsunjia Village, Datong County, Qinghai Province, presents a cheerful scene of 5,000 years ago.

prayer for rain in the time of drought; *The Music of Yinkang Clan*, a musical dance for health and well-being; *The Music of Yiqi Clan*, a prayer for a good harvest at the Laji Festival (a festival for offering sacrifices at the end of the year); and *The Music of Getian Clan*, a description of the lives of primitive people during the first years of agricultural production. The second type of primitive music dance celebrated the exploits of legendary ancient emperors, including Emperor Huangdi, Zhuan Xu, Emperor Ku, Emperor Yao and Emperor Shun. It is said that the tribe of Emperor Huangdi regarded clouds as totems, which inspired the music dance *Yunmen Dajuan*. *Shao* was the dance music created to praise the Emperor Shun. According to records, this involved musical instruments playing "nine-chapter Xiaoshao" and "striking stones," and performances in which people acted like "running birds and beasts" and "dancing animals."

"Cutting bamboo, making bamboo into bows, throwing clay and hitting beasts." This is from *The Tan Song*, a song believed to be written in the period of the Emperor Huangdi and recorded in *The Annals of Wu and Yue in the Spring and Autumn Period*. It is thought to be the earliest known example of poetry in China and describes how people made tools to go hunting and fishing. Using simple and rhythmic language it records this process in detail, from making bows to hunting animals.

In *Lü's Spring and Autumn Annals*, the chapter on ancient musical instruments contains a vivid description of singing and dancing in ancient China: "People in the Getian Clan usually dance and sing for recreation. Three people would hold the cattle's tails, dancing and singing merrily, and eight songs were sung." The eight songs mentioned were: *Zaimin*, a song praising the earth that carried both the sky and people; *Xuanniao*, a song about the auspicious black bird, a totem that the clan worshipped; *Sui Caomu*, a song about trees and grass; *Fen Wugu*, a song used to pray for grain harvests; *Jing Tianchang*, to extol the gifts from the gods; *Da Digong*, a song extending thanks to the kindness of the gods; *Yi Dide*, a song thanking mother earth; and the *Zongqinshou Zhiji*, a song to pray to the gods for more animals and a stable and happy life. As this suggests, music dances of this period reflect on the challenges of everyday life and the delicate relationship between man and nature.

Much of the literature describing activities in the primitive period not only records the forms of music extant at that time, but also some of the musical instruments available. For instance, in *Lü's Spring and Autumn Annals*, a chapter on ancient musical instruments describes a time in the history of the Zhuxiang Clan when there were extremely harsh climatic conditions, including strong winds and heavy sand storms, which resulted in little vegetation and fruitless plants. A member of the Zhuxiang Clan invented a *se* (a type of musical instrument) with five chords to pray for rain. This five-chord *se* is perhaps the most representative musical instrument of the primitive period.

The Xia, Shang and Western Zhou Dynasties

The Xia Dynasty (2070–1600 BC) saw the beginning of the development of Chinese society from primitive conditions. The music dances, previously devoted to totemic sacrifices, were now used to extol monarchies or the achievements of kings. For example, the music of *Daxia* praised the exploits of Dayu who successfully regulated the water system during the Xia Dynasty: "He worked hard day and night, digging mountain earth to block up dike breaches," "all for the interests of people." The music dance *Dawei* in the Shang Dynasty (1600–1046 BC) was created to offer sacrifices to the ancestors and to celebrate the success of Cheng Tang who defeated Jie, the last ruler of the Xia Dynasty.

It was during the Shang Dynasty that Chinese civilization entered the Bronze Age. As the craft and bronze-smelting sectors developed, more than ten percussion instruments and blowpipes were invented. They included a single *qing* or a set of *qing*s (consisting of three *qing*s and producing low or high-pitched sounds), as well as bell-like percussion instruments such as *nao* that were placed on shelves, *duo* and *ling* that were held and struck by hand, and hanging bells and *yong* that produced sounds when struck. Among them, bells and *qing*s had the most far-reaching influence on the music of later generations.

The bells, made of bronze giving a loud and solemn sound, were called "gold"—one of the eight fundamental sounds in ancient Chinese music. *Qing*, made of *qing* stones that produce a clear and piercing sound, were called "stones." The combination of bells and *qing*s is thus said to produce "the sound of gold and stones." This combination of sounds is often referred to in ancient books and poems: "the sound of bells and *qing*s would shock the mountains and rivers" and "striking bells and *qing*s while raising flags." Bells and *qing*s were regarded as ritual instruments and would be played on such important occasions as setting off for battle, going to the imperial court, offering sacrifices or grand feasts.

Chinese "ritual music" originated from primitive worship in ancient times. "Playing music by beating earthen drums," as recorded in *The Book of Rites*, constitutes the earliest form of ritual music. Yet despite its presence and dramatic development in the Xia and Shang dynasties, this ritual music was considered to be a supplement to religious and political events. Some scholars have characterized the Xia culture as "one of obeying fates" and the Shang culture as "one of honoring the gods." In the Western Zhou Dynasty (1046–771 BC), however, the political implications of "obeying the gods' will" were weakened greatly. The Duke of Zhou restructured and organized the ritual music created from ancient times to the Shang Dynasty, and developed it into a set of systematic social rules and codes of conduct. Also, special organizations were established to standardize and manage the performance of music dances. The *Dasiyue* was one of

A special stone *qing* excavated from the Yin Ruins in Anyang, Henan Province.

the organizations responsible for teaching royal families, nobles and some talented commoners music. This course of instruction included "music morals," "music languages" and "music dances" (detailed in *The Rites of the Zhou*).

A bronze drum from the Shang Dynasty unearthed in Chongyang, Hubei Province.

The music dances, previously performed to extol totems and ancestors, were changed into a form suitable for performance at feasts and during sacrificial activities. There were many different types of music in the Zhou Dynasty, with records dating back to the twenty-ninth year of the reign of Duke Xiang in *The Annals of Zuo*.

The court ritual music system in the Western Zhou Dynasty was very rigid. For example, officials of different positions could only retain music dance groups that were equivalent to their ranks in feast entertainment. The types and numbers

Xun from the Shang Dynasty unearthed in Huixian County, Henan Province.

of musical instruments, lines and numbers of dance groups, as well as categories and numbers of musicians for kings and nobles were also strictly enforced and could not be mixed.

The supreme form of hierarchal music in the Zhou Dynasty was the *Liu Dai Yue Wu (Six-dynasty Yue Wu)*, or *Six Pieces of Music*. After defeating King Zhou, King Wu of the Zhou Dynasty asked Duke Dan of Zhou to create a new kind of ritual music. The *Six Dances* and *Six Little Dances* are important examples of this music. The *Six Dances*, or *Liu Bu Yue Wu (Six-part Music Dance)*, was used mainly as one of the sacrificial rites in the court of the Zhou Dynasty. As such, it was performed regularly before the king and featured grand scenes and a great number of participants. It consisted of six dances, including the *Yunmen* used to honor heaven, *Daxian* to honor mother earth, *Dashao* for the worship of mountains and rivers at a distance, *Daxia* for the gods and spirits in mountains and rivers, *Dahuo* for female ancestors and *Dawu* for male ancestors. The *Six Pieces of Music* was also called the *Six-dynasty Yue Wu*, as it was primarily composed of the

A large bell with a pattern of clouds excavated from Taiyuan, Shanxi Province.

representative music dances of dynasties prior to the Zhou Dynasty.

The *Six Little Dances* was used to teach the children of aristocrats music dance and, at times, was also used during sacrificial activities. It included *Fuwu* (dancing with long sticks decorated with colorful silk ribbons), *Yuwu* (dancing with feathers), *Huangwu* (dancing with colorful bird feathers), *Maowu* (dancing with ox tails) and *Ganwu* (also called *Bingwu*, dancing with shields). After the Qin Dynasty, the *Six-dynasty Music Dance* was restricted to *Shao* music (civil music) and *Wu* music (martial music). *Shao* and *Wu* were the most important types of music played in the imperial courts of all dynasties, and the former, as the ritual music of the supreme hierarchal level, was played until the end of the Qing Dynasty (1644–1911).

In the Shang and Zhou dynasties, China was among the world's biggest powers. It also boasted a highly developed music culture. The *qing* and drum orchestra were popular in the Shang Dynasty, while the bell and *qing* orchestra, featuring chime bells and chime *qing*s, were used in the Zhou Dynasty. In addition, the presence and use of the *Six-Dynasty Music Dance*, the invention of various kinds of new musical instruments, and advances in composition such as *yuelü* (music rhythm), all showed that Chinese music had come of age.

The Zhou Dynasty also had an active folk music culture. Many musical stories that are still told today, such as *Boya met his close friend Zhong Ziqi by playing the Qin*, have their roots in this period. The development of this strong folk music tradition can be attributed to improvements in instrument playing, composition and the musical appreciation of the general populace. Historical records are full of praise for performers of this period. For example, praise was heaped upon ancient *qin* players for their superb mastery of the instrument. At the time, this was attributed to their true and deep feelings. It was also said that the singing of the famous

Pentatonic scale
This is the collective name of five musical scales: do, re, mi, so and la. All the traditional Chinese scale forms include the said five scales. Various modes might be formed based on each tone that is considered the principal tone in a sequence of music tones consisting of the pentatonic scale. According to the scale names of the principal tones, modes could fall into different categories, such as do-mode, re-mode, mi-mode, so-mode and la-mode.

musician Qin Qing in the Zhou Dynasty could "shock the trees and stop clouds from moving," and the singing of the folk singer Han E could "linger in the mind for a long time."

It was during the Zhou Dynasty that the theory of twelve *lüs* and the names of the "pentatonic scale," known as *gong, shang, jue, zhi* and *yu*, were established. One of the outstanding achievements in the theory of *lü* was the *Sanfen Sunyi* method recorded in the *Guanzi Di Yuan*.

The Spring and Autumn Period and the Warring States Period

The Spring and Autumn Period (770–476 BC) saw the rise of regional music because of the collapse of long-established religious and legal customs (such as passing the throne to the elder son of the legal wife rather than the son of concubines, and the fiefdom system). In the Warring States Period, numerous wars also led to frequent collaborations between composers and musicians from different regional music traditions. Ancient musical instruments unearthed in 1978 from the tomb of Marquis Yi of the State of Zeng in Suixian County (present-day Suizhou), Hubei, provide important evidence that such collaborations were an important feature of regional music-making in this period.

"Sanfen Sunyi" method
This was one of the ancient Chinese *lü* generation methods. Guan Zhong in the Spring and Autumn Period invented the *Sanfen Sunyi* Method that was used to figure out the length of *lü* for the pentatonic scale. The same or similar *lü* generation methods also appeared in ancient Greek and Arabic countries. Based on length of the vibrating bodies, the *Sanfen Sunyi* method included two aspects: *sanfen sunyi* and *sanfen yiyi*. Cutting one-third from a certain chord meant *sanfen sunyi*, which could result in the upper fifth of the chord tone; increasing the chord by one-third meant *sanfen yiyi*, which generated the lower quarter of the chord tone. Alteration and consecutive use of the said two methods would generate all music *lüs* based on the first *lü*. The earliest record of the *Sanfen Sunyi* method ever known was in *Guanzi: Di Yuan*, in which there were only five tones; while the records in *Lü's Spring and Autumn Annals: Yinlü* showed that the method had figured out all the length codes of the 12 *lüs*. The method by which the *lü* of the upper fifth was calculated based on the sequence of the *Sanfen Sunyi* method was called *xiasheng* in ancient times, and the method in which the lower quarter was calculated was called *shangsheng*. Twelve *lüs* were finally generated with five *xiasheng lüs* and six *shangsheng lüs*.

Chime bells excavated from the tomb of Marquis Yi. The bells standing in the north are 3.35 meters long and 2.73 meters tall; while the bells in the west are 7.48 meters long and 2.65 meters tall.

In his book *Chinese History*, Guo Moruo shows that in the states of Sui and Zeng, there were marquises that had the same family names as marquises in the Zhou Dynasty. The inscriptions on the unearthed bronze show that marquises of the State of Zeng were formerly a branch of the main Zhou Dynasty. The sixty-five-piece chime bell discovered in the tomb of Marquis Yi is the most complete and biggest bronze chime bell known so far. Chimes

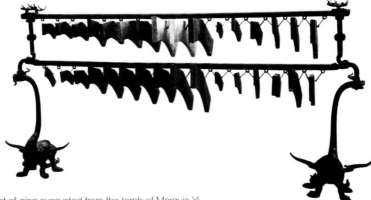

A set of *qing* excavated from the tomb of Marquis Yi measures 1.09 meters long and 2.15 meters tall.

Figurines of performers and dancers excavated from a tomb of the Warring States Period in Zhangqiu, Shandong Province.

appeared as early as the Shang Dynasty, with three to five bells at first, nine to thirteen in the Zhou Dynasty, and sixty-one in the Warring States Period.

The period from the Zhou Dynasty to the Warring States Period saw richer categories of musical instruments, more refined instrument-making skills, and enhanced requirements of sound quality. The making of musical instruments used in playing *yayue* (elegant music), such as chime bells and chime *qing*s, involved a great deal of labor and money. The chime bells unearthed from the tomb of Marquis Yi boast five octaves, only one octave less than the sound range of modern pianos. The bells would produce beautiful and pure sounds when struck, with chords the same as the modern C Major.

The "eight sound" classification method was adopted for musical instruments at this time. This method was used to classify musical instruments into eight categories based on the materials used to make them: gold (bronze bell and *bo* or big bell), stone (stone *qing*, a percussion instrument), earth (ceramic *xun*, a wind instrument, and *fou*, a percussion instrument), leather (*tao* drums), silk (*qin* and *se* with chords made of silk), wood (wooden percussion instruments like *zhu* and *yu*), *pao* (*sheng* and *yu*, whose bases are made of gourds) and bamboo (*xiao* and *chi*, wind instruments).

The Qin and Han Dynasties

The Qin Dynasty (221–206 BC), as a centralized empire, was the first to establish an official organization—a music institute—devoted to the management of music for political and cultural purposes. The need for unification resulted in the continuance of the official collation of folk music, which had started during the Zhou Dynasty. The organization was responsible for collecting, organizing and adapting folk music, and groups of musicians were arranged to perform on such occasions as feasts, sacrifices and other celebrations.

The music institute was developed further during the Han Dynasty (206BC–220AD). Emperor Wudi of the Han Dynasty paid particular attention to folk music and expanded the organization and functions of the music institute. He ordered the collection of the folk songs of ethnic groups in various areas, including Beidi and remote areas like the western regions of China. This collection included *Shen Lai Yan Yi* (*Entertaining the gods at a banquet when they came*), *Cheng Xuan Si Long* (*Riding on Dragons*), *Anshi*

A figure of a *xun* performer from the Western Han Dynasty.

Performing, Singing and Dancing Gods unearthed from a painted coffin in the tombs of the Western Han Dynasty at Mawangdui.

Fangzhong Yue (*The Boudoir Poetry of the Peaceful Age*), and *Jiaosi Yue* (*The Music for Rural Sacrifice*). The *Jiaosi Yue* is particularly noteworthy as it was accompanied by a magnificently dressed shamen who sang while dancing gracefully in the moonlight. When performed, this could be heard everywhere from the suburbs of Chang'an to the front hall and living quarters of the imperial court. Most of the music collected by the institute conveyed a romantic and splendid world of immortals, as was reflected in *The Nine Songs* of Qu Yuan. In addition, there were improvised songs that were chiefly concerned with matters of everyday life, such as *Song of the Great Wind* and other folk songs from around the country.

The most famous form of music associated with the Han Dynasty music institute was *Xianghe Ge* (*Songs of Harmony*). Early *Xianghe Ge* featured "one singing and three others echoing." It later developed to be performed with such musical instruments as the *si* and *zhu*. *The Ode to Shanglin*, written by Sima Xiangru, describes a typical performance provided by the music institute in the time of the Western Han Dynasty. After returning from hunting, the emperor held a banquet on the towering terrace. Huge chimes below the terrace were struck and huge divine drums—*tuo* drums—decorated with feathers were beaten. The music was created by the singing and echoing of a great number of people. The sound was powerful enough to shake both the mountains and rivers. The singers and dancers, like the beautiful legendary fairies Qing Qin and Mi Fei, were performing music dances of ancient times like *Shao*, *Huo*, *Wu* and *Xiang*, as well as those of different styles from various parts of the country. Also, many miraculous performances by *paiyou* (ancient clowns), *homunculi* and *xiangren* (performers wearing animal masks) coming from the Western regions were arranged, which brought great joy and entertainment to the people.

The Han Dynasty also saw the popularity of *guchui* music (drum and wind music). This type of music was either performed on horses or in a parade and was used on such occasions as military ceremonies and court banquets. *Guchui* music was closely associated with folk songs and featured love songs and anti-war themed works. Such was the influence of *guchui*, these themes even infused the military music of the Han Dynasty, including *Shangye* (a piece of *nao* music) that praised the eternity of love, and *Ziliuma* (a piece of *hengchui* music) whose words include, "joining the army at 15 and returning at the age of 80."

The Period of the Three Kingdoms, the Western and Eastern Jin Dynasties and the Southern and Northern Dynasties

The period of the Three Kingdoms, the Western and Eastern Jin Dynasties and the Southern and Northern Dynasties (220–581 AD) was one of turbulence caused by frequent wars. It also witnessed unprecedented cultural exchanges among all nations, and dramatic progress in Chinese music. The Silk Road, a collection of trade routes established during the Han Dynasty, facilitated the introduction of music to the inner lands of the western regions. In the eighteenth year of the reign of Emperor Jianyuan in the pre-Qin Dynasty (382 AD), Lü Guang introduced *qiuci* (now called kucha in Xinjiang) music to the inner lands and called it "*qinhanji*," integrating it further with the music of the Shaanxi and Gansu areas.

Buddhism spread quickly in China during this period. As a result, *Fanbei*, a form of regional Chinese Buddhist folk music, grew in popularity. The art of playing and composing for the ancient *qin* also made significant progress. A group of scholarly *qin* artists like Ji Kang and Ruan Ji established their reputations with such well-known songs as *Guangling*

A brick with the figure of a *qin* performer excavated from a tomb of the Wei and Jin dynasties in Jiuquan, Gansu Province.

A brick with figures of flute players unearthed from a Southern Dynasty tomb at Dengxian County, Henan Province.

San and *Jiukuang*. The popularity of these songs shifted Chinese music towards the concepts of harmony and beauty. *Guangling San*, previously a form of folk instrumental music from the Guangling area (current Yangzhou, Jiangsu) in the Han Dynasty, was adapted as a song played with the ancient *qin* in the late Eastern Han Dynasty, and became more popular in the Three Kingdoms Period when Ji Kang performed the piece. The music describes a moving story about Nie Zheng, the son of a sword-casting craftsman in the Warring States Period, who stabbed the king of the State of Han in revenge for his father's death and then killed himself to protect his mother. With an exciting and passionate melody, *Guangling San* is one of the rare grand pieces of music played on the ancient *qin* and is of great artistic value.

Qingshang music, based on *Xiang He Ge*, gained great attention from the Cao Wei Regime in the northern areas, which resulted in the establishment of the Qingshang Institute. *Qingshang* music combined various styles of music from the Han and Wei dynasties and was the umbrella term for *jiyue*, a type of music based on the folk music of that time. Also called *Qingshang Qu*, it was generally performed on occasions such as banquets as entertainment for the upper social class. The *Qingshang Qu* music could always be guaranteed attention from the imperial courts of all dynasties. The turmoil of wars in the Western Jin and Eastern Jin dynasties led to *Qingshang* music spreading to the southern areas of China and becoming further integrated with *Wu Ge* and *Xi Qu* (two music forms). In the Northern Wei Dynasty, *Qingshang* music once again returned to the northern areas and became one of the dominant forces in Chinese music.

The Sui and Tang Dynasties

The Sui and Tang dynasties provided very different conditions from those that preceded them. Political stability, a thriving economy and the open cultural policies adopted by rulers, led to an integration of the diverse music cultures of all ethnic groups that had not been seen since the Wei and Jin dynasties. During this period, music of all ethnic groups and even some foreign folk music were collectively called "Seven-part Music" or "Nine-part Music." Everyone, from royal families, nobles and officials to ordinary people, was able to enjoy and contribute to the music of this period.

Dance music in the Tang Dynasty integrated instrumental music, songs and dances. It included such outstanding works as *Pozhen Yue* (*The Music of Breaking up the Enemy's Front*, also known as *The Music of the King Qin Breaking up the Enemy's Front*) and *Nishang Yuyi Qu* (*Song of Rainbow Skirts and Feather Robes*). The latter work was compiled by Emperor Xuanzong of Tang. It was an adaptation of *Poluomen Qu*, dedicated to the emperor by Yang Jinshu, a military commander (*Jiedushi*) in the Hexi area.

The Tang Dynasty also saw the establishment of a series of music management and educational organizations. Taichang Temple

A figurine of a *kugo* performer of the Sui Dynasty.

Painting of Musical Performance, a colored relief sculpture made of white marble from the Five Dynasties was excavated from the tomb of Wang Chuzhi in Quyan, Hebei Province. Female performers play musical instruments of various types with rapt expressions.

was the supreme organization responsible for ritual music; the Education Institute was established especially for training musicians; the Guchui Institute for military music; and Dayue Institute as a musical education organization for *yayue* and *yanyue* musicians. These organizations were responsible for training a large group of talented artists.

Quzi, a form of folk music, emerged during the Sui and Tang dynasties. It includes the folk songs of the Han and other ethnic groups. *Quzi* music became very fashionable with musicians at this time and it even became popular to add new lyrics. Tang poems, among the great achievements of Chinese literature, were an obvious accompaniment to *quzi* music. This collaboration between the worlds of music and poetry was mutually beneficial. Singers in the Tang Dynasty were delighted to sing lines written by well-known poets, and poets took pride in the fact that their work had been turned into song. There is a famous story from this period about three poets: Wang Zhihuan, Gao Shi and Wang Changling were all renowned at that time. Well matched in their talent for poetry, they were also good friends. One day they

A mural painting in the Mogao Grottoes in Dunhuang presents a lively performing and dancing scene. The *pipa* (lute) player in the middle performs the stunt of playing a Chinese *pipa* from the reverse side.

went to a wine shop together where they encountered a group of musicians. They agreed that the person whose poems were most frequently sung by the musicians would be the one who enjoyed the greatest fame. Later, a musician sang two poems of Wang Changling, and another sang one of Gao Shi's. Wang Zhihuan said, "They sang the songs that could only be heard by their own villagers. Let's wait and see!" Sure enough, an attractive singer rose to sing, "Where the Yellow River flows from the white clouds/ An isolated city is there surrounded by ten-thousand-foot mountains/ Why do you play the lament *Breaking Willows* with *qiangdi?* / Spring breeze never blows through the Jade Pass." This was the new work of Wang Zhihuan. Upon hearing the song, the three poets couldn't help but laugh together.

The *pipa* was one of the most important musical instruments adopted by orchestras during the Tang Dynasty. In fact, the *pipa* of the Tang dynasty was almost the same as the *pipa* that is used today. The *nanqu*, played in Fujian, and the Japanese *pipa* have also

Figurines of lute and pan flute performers on horse back from the Tang Dynasty.

kept some of the traits of the *pipa* of the Tang Dynasty, both in form and in ways of playing. Innovations in music theory during the Tang Dynasty were influenced by *qiuci* music and included music theories such as the "eighty-four modulations" and the "twenty-eight modulations." It was also during the Tang Dynasty that Cao Rou created the ancient *qin* music notation that is still used today.

The musical activities held in the courts and the houses of official families were colorful and splendid, reflecting both innovations based on traditional culture and the incorporation of new foreign music forms. They included not only large-scale elegant music dances for royal courts, but also performances combining music, dances and poetry. Cultural exchanges and the integration of traditional and foreign cultures reached a level during the Tang Dynasty that had never been seen before. This led to many cultural and musical innovations that illustrated an open-mindedness and willingness to change, making the Tang Dynasty one of the richest cultural periods of Chinese feudal society.

The Song and Yuan Dynasties

The urban economic boom experienced during the Song Dynasty (960–1279) led to the emergence of *goulan*, *washe* and other entertainment venues that catered to the cultural lives of the people. The *goulan* or *washe* were full of noise and different types of entertainment: cries of hawkers, singing in the *piaochang* or *changzhuan* styles, and performances on *guzici*, *zhugongdiao* and *zaju*. These were entirely new music forms, marking a new milestone for popular folk music. The period was described by some as one that saw "music's shift from court to civil society, from aristocrats to ordinary civilians, and the representative form of music from dances to opera."

The Song Dynasty witnessed the emergence of numerous excellent *quzi*s, which inherited the strengths of those of the Sui Dynasty, and a large group of writers of *ci* and *qu* (poetry and music).

Goulan and washe
Goulan in the Song Dynasty was mostly associated with *washe*. *Washe* (also called "*washi*" or *wazi*) were places offering all sorts of entertainment in ancient Chinese cities, and the major performance centers for operas in the Song and Yuan dynasties, the equivalent to today's theaters.

Piaochang and changzhuan
Piaochang was a type of singing based on changing the cadences and tunes of music and lyrics that already existed. *Changzhuan* adapted some popular songs. Opening words would be added to the front and epilogue in the back within the same musical tone, with the same lyrics adopted throughout the whole song.

Detail from the *Painting of Singer and Performer Figures* from the Southern Song Dynasty.

Guzici, zhugongdiao and zaju
Guzici and *zhugongdiao* were
the major forms of "telling
and singing music" in the
Song and Yuan dynasties.
Guzici referred to a type of
music in which a piece of
music was sung repeatedly,
with storytelling added
into the singing process.
Zhugongdiao was first created
by Kong Sanchuan, an artist
in Goulan, Bianjing during the
Northern Song Dynasty. The
music structure consisted of
connecting many pieces of
music of the same musical
tone into a full set, and
adding many sets of different
musical tones or single pieces
of music together to describe
a long story with singing
and telling forms. "*Zaju*"
and Southern Opera were
emerging opera styles in the
Song and Yuan dynasties. *Zaju*
was from the northern areas.
By inheriting the traditions of
dances and military operas of
the Tang Dynasty, *zaju*, based
on *quzi*, reached its peak in
the Yuan Dynasty following
its earlier development in
the Song and Jin dynasties.
Performances of *zaju* in the
Song Dynasty consisted of
three parts including *yanduan*,
zhengzaju and *sanduan*.
Yanduan involved ordinary
experiences; *sanduan*
included humorous stories,
but only *zhengzaju* was real
story-telling opera.

Well-known writers in these two art forms included
Liu Yong, Zhou Bangyan, Jiang Kui, and Zhang Yan,
and their works included songs like *To the Tune of
Yangzhou Man*, *Apricot Blossoms against a Blue Sky* and
To the Tune of Plums along the Ge River.

Since the Han and Tang dynasties, ancient *qin* music
had become increasingly the preserve of scholars.
Also, different genres took shape based on different
performance arts, with Guo Chuwang from the
Zhejiang genre the most outstanding representative.

Chinese opera came of age in the Song Dynasty,
which was marked by the presence of Southern Opera
in the Southern Song Dynasty (1127–1279). From the
late Northern Song Dynasty (960–1127) to the Southern
Song Dynasty, a form of opera—the Southern Opera,
or *xiwen*—developed in Wenzhou in the southern areas
of China. With marked differences from *zaju* in the
Song Dynasty, it was all about performing stories with
diverse structures accompanied by music dominated

Painting of Musical Performance, a mural painting discovered from the tomb
chamber of Zhang Kuang, tomb No. 10 of a grave from the Liao Dynasty in
Xuanhua, Hebei Province. The picture depicts the informal *gagaku* music that
prevailed in the Song Dynasty. It could be performed in a variety of ways and be
accompanied by a band.

Mural painting depicting Yuan operas.

by *xiaoqus* and ballads that were popular in the southern areas. The music later developed as the *qupaiti* style of opera and further into the *jiqu* form consisting of many *yueju* with different *qupai*s. Southern Opera came in various singing forms, including solo, choral and chorus singing.

In the early Yuan Dynasty (1271–1368), the styles of both Southern and Northern Opera were established. Northern

Opera music was dominated by the heptatonic scale and was deep and magnificent. In contrast, Southern Opera music was dominated by the pentatonic scale and was tender and elegant. It was also during the Yuan Dynasty that a completely new form of opera appeared. Performed in conjunction with Northern Opera, *zaju* came with a play, integrated singing, voice-over narration, dances, and included a combination of verse and prose. The creation of such classic works as *The Injustice to Dou E* by Guan Hanqing and *The Romance of the Western Chamber* by Wang Shifu marked the peak of the *zaju* in the Yuan Dynasty. This also reflected the fact that Chinese music had surpassed common expressions of feelings and had become more focused on revealing human nature and manifesting the inner worlds of various kinds of people.

The Ming and Qing Dynasties

The Ming and Qing dynasties (1368–1911) saw the dawn of capitalism in Chinese society. With an increasingly citizen class, the music culture of this time tended to be more secularized and further enriched the lives of ordinary people. The Ming Dynasty (1368–1644) boasted a diverse range of folk songs that, though somewhat vulgar, had such extensive influence that everyone, male or female, could sing them. In the meantime, private workshops started to collect, edit and publish folk songs, resulting in published booklets of lyrics, opera scripts and *qin* music scores becoming available, including *Mountains Songs* edited by Feng Menglong, and the earliest *qin* music, *The Mysterious and Marvellous Tablatures of the Qin* edited by Zhu Quan.

"Telling and singing music" came in a variety of forms in the Ming and Qing dynasties, including *tanci guci* as well as *paiziqu*, *qinshu* and *daoqing*. The *tanci* in Suzhou had the biggest influence

Yueluquanshu, a 40-volume book written by Zhu Zaiyu, currently in the collection of the National Museum of China.

in the southern areas, while *guci* music such as the big drums in Shandong, Xihe and Beijing, and the wooden drum in Jizhong, were the most famous and influential pieces of music in the northern areas. The *paiziqu* music included *danxian* and *dadiaoquzi* in Henan; *qinshu* music was represented by *qinshu* in Shandong and *yangqin* in Sichuan; *daoqing* music included the *daoqing* in Zhejiang and Shaanxi, and *yugu* in Hubei. Some ethnic groups also had their own forms of "telling and singing music" like the story-telling of Mongolian tribes and *dabaiqu* of the Bai ethnic group.

The period saw another peak in operatic music marked by the "four major tunes" (*Haiyan, Yuyao, Yiyang* and *Kunshan*). The *Kunshan* tune, redeveloped by musicians like Wei Liangfu in Jiangsu, gained popularity for its pleasant and smooth melody as well as highlights on pronunciation. Through the integration of southern and northern opera music, the *Kunshan* tune was later developed into Kun opera that was popular with the people. The *Yiyang* tune heavily influenced local dialect opera music with its flexible and changing style, leading to an increasing number of local operas. In the northern areas, the *bangzi* tune represented by the *qin* tune in Shaanxi developed rapidly. High-pitched and unconstrained, the *bangzi* tune had lasting and far-reaching influences. In the late Qing Dynasty, the *pihuang* tune, consisting of two basic melodies known as *xipi* and *erhuang*, initially took shape and further evolved into the Peking Opera that has become popular throughout the country.

Orchestral music that combined multiple musical instruments appeared during the Ming and Qing dynasties. This included the pipe music played in the Zhihua Temple in Beijing, *chuige* in Hebei, *sizhu* in the areas south of the Yangtze River and Shifan luogu. *Qin* music, like *Wild Geese over the Clam Sands* in the Ming Dynasty and *Flowing Water* in the Qing Dynasty, were widely spread, popular works. Well-known pieces of *pipa* music included *Haiqing Hunting the Swan* and *Ambush on Ten Sides*, created during the period from the late Yuan Dynasty to early Ming Dynasty. It was also during the Qing Dynasty that the *Tablature of the Pipa* was compiled by Hua Qiuping, the first work of its kind.

A figurine of a cymbal performer on horseback from the Ming Dynasty.

The Ming Dynasty produced an eminent *yuelü* expert, Zhu Zaiyu, who was the first person to establish the theory of "equal temperament." By calculating the length proportion between any two neighboring *Lü* (semitones) in equal temperament (with

A painting from the Qing Dynasty portrays female performers playing *erhus* and south bangs.

the accuracy of 25 digits), the theory was a revolution in both music and the physics of music, and a milestone in the history of civilization.

After 1840

China underwent a series of anti-imperialist and anti-feudal revolutions following the Opium War of 1840. For the first time, there were attempts to introduce new western music from Europe as a companion to, or even replacement for, traditional Chinese music.

An interior view of an opera house in Beijing in the late Qing Dynasty. (Collected by Wang Shucun)

Societies that aimed to promote and encourage the use of traditional musical instruments for all members of society were also founded at this time, including the Tianyun Society and Datong Musical Society. Folk music activities resulted in numerous outstanding artists, among whom the most well known was Hua Yanjun—also known as Xiazi Abing ("the blind Abing")—who was most famous for the plaintive and touching performance of *The Moon Reflected on the Er-quan Spring (Er Quan Ying Yue)*.

Peking Opera developed its unique character during this period and had extensive influence throughout the country, with the emergence of a number of excellent opera masters such as Cheng Changgeng, Tan Xinpei and Mei Lanfang, Cheng Yanqiu and Zhou Xinfang. Meanwhile, local operas such as the Ping Opera, Yue Opera and Chu Opera also grew in importance and popularity.

The School Song was one of the most influential western music styles introduced to China from the late Qing Dynasty to the early Republic of China. Most of the School Songs included lyrics based on foreign music, but some adopted elements of native music as well. Influenced by the New Culture Movement of the 1910s and 1920s, there was a drive to improve traditional Chinese music by introducing both western musical styles and associated western values such as science and democracy. This led to the creation of a

New Youth—A periodical during the New Culture Movement.

number of new musical societies. They included the Music Research Society of Peking University, the Chinese Aesthetics Education Society and the National Music Improvement Society. In the 1920s, Xiao Youmei founded the National Music Institute in Shanghai, which marked the start of professional and formal music education in China. Other representatives of the movement included Zhao Yuanren, Huang Zi, Wang Guangqi, Liu Tianhua and Li Jinhui.

The composer Zhao Yuanren became famous during the "May Fourth Movement" period (1915–1921) as one of the main representatives of early professional music creation in China. He focused on combining language with the tunes of folk songs and was good at integrating the strengths of traditional music with well-known works such as *Cloth Seller's Song* and *How Could I*

Not Think of Her. Huang Zi, the music educator and composer, also contributed a considerable amount to professional music education by training numerous musicians (including Liu Xuean, Jiang Dingxian and He Luting) and composing such popular music as *Three Wishes of the Rose*. He also composed China's first cantata, *Song of Everlasting Sorrow*. The musician Liu Tianhua explored how to improve native Chinese music by learning from the western musical tradition and established the National Music Improvement Society. He also composed *erhu* solos like *Song of a Bright Future, Birds Singing in Silent Mountains* and *Moaning in Sickness*, and made *erhu* music an important part of professional music education.

In terms of creating music that integrated more Chinese features, Li Jinhui was a pioneer who composed a large number of operas for children including *The Little Painter, The Sparrow and Children* and *Poor Qiuxiang*. His popular works included *Little Rain* and *Dear Girl, I Love You*, works that established him as the father of modern Chinese popular music. Wang Guangqi, another important musician of this period, made pioneering contributions to Chinese music history and comparative music study.

During the War of Resistance against Japan (1937–1945), an incredible number of new musical works sprang up reflecting the spirit of the time. Various musical genres, including symphony, chorus, opera and music for the piano and violin, were also

A statue of Xiao Youmei—the pioneer and founder of modern music education in China.

transformed. Musicians like Xian Xinghai, Nie Er, He Luting, Ma Sicong and Lü Ji made significant contributions to the development of Chinese music. Important works composed and performed in this period include *On the Songhua River* by Zhang Hanhui, *Song of the Great Wall* by Liu Xuean, *My Hometown* by Lu Huabo and *On the Jialing River* by He Luting.

After the formation of the People's Republic of China in 1949, the Maoist government suppressed popular music and encouraged the creation of revolutionary works. Significant works of this period include the large-scale dance epic *The East Is Red*, the film music *Liu Sanjie*, the opera *Red Guards on Honghu Lake* and the violin concerto *Butterfly Lovers*. The development of Chinese music was interrupted in later periods due to strict ideological restrictions, particularly those imposed during the Cultural Revolution (1966-1976). China's reform since 1978 has brought Chinese musical culture back on track, resulting in a boom in every aspect of music, including composition, performance, education, theory and marketing.

Chapter 2
The Meaning of Ancient
Music of China

Traditional Chinese culture is largely based on rural values. It emphasizes the harmony of nature, harmony between human beings and nature, harmony between human beings and society, harmony between human beings, and harmony between the body and the heart. According to traditional Chinese philosophy, the lives of human beings are in coordination and unity with other lives in the universe, meaning that they are in harmony with each other. Hui Shi, who was the first to propose this idea, said that "Human beings should treat natural lives in an equal way, because they are closely linked with each other."

Harmony between human beings and nature was the highest goal of the ancient sages. For this reason, Chinese music adopted nature as its first theme. The famous *guqin* song *Lofty Mountains and Flowing Water* attempts to give listeners the impression of high mountains and flowing rivers. This attempt to simulate nature in music is quite different from that found in western music. In *Lofty Mountains and Flowing Water*, the musician and the mountains and water are as one, since the musician's emotions are embodied in the music. The same commitment to harmony is reflected in the landscape paintings and poems of ancient China. Since humans are in harmony with nature, they have become a part of nature, rather than a detached spectator or observer.

In fact, most traditional Chinese songs, including *Spring Flowers in the Moonlit Night on the River*, *Fishermen Singing at Dusk*, *Wild Geese over the Clam Sands* and *Three Variations of Plum Blossoms*, *Autumn Moon over the Calm Lake*, and *The Moon Reflected on the Er-quan Spring*, do not only aim to describe natural scenes. They all attempt to provide musical examples of harmony between human beings and nature.

The ideologists of the pre-Qin period thought that music had a close relationship with nature, human beings and society. It was a kind of culture with profound natural and social significance. Both the Confucian ideas of rites and music, and the Taoist concept of pursuing harmony between human beings and nature were established on the concept that music is the expression of the harmony between human beings and nature. In this way, music is connected with nature and society. Taoists advocate appreciating the beauty of nature, thus putting forward the view that the sounds of nature are the best music. Confucians consider music as a tool for adjusting emotions and cultivating morality. It shoulders the responsibility of civilizing the people, evaluating political gains and losses, and coordinating social and ethical orders as part of the Confucian ritual system. In addition, there is another influential musical ideal from Buddhism, which teaches that opening one's mind is essential to the appreciation of music.

Propriety and Music in Confucianism

Propriety is the generic term for the rites related to daily lives and social activities, which are used as codes of conduct for human behavior. The Duke of Zhou called for making rites and music at the same time, aiming to civilize people through discipline and self-discipline. Music could be used to adjust the

Painting of Sage's Traces from the Ming Dynasty portrays a scene where Confucius talks about music with the Grand Tutor of the Kingdom of *Qi*. He was said to be obsessed with *Shao*, a type of music popular during the reign of Emperor Shundi.

temperament of people, while rites could be used to regulate the behavior of the people. Therefore, people would be willing to obey social and ethical codes and behave in a proper way. Society would then be stable and people would live peaceful lives.

It is said that Confucius once listened to *shao* music, which was so wonderful that he did not know the taste of meat for three months. Confucius valued music very highly. He stated, "It is by the Odes that the mind is aroused. It is by the Rules of Propriety that the character is established. It is from Music that the finish is received." In his opinion, music was an important part of developing a majestic personality and enhancing morality. He believed music could play an important role in self-cultivation and safeguarding the stability of a state.

According to the *Analects · Shu Er,* when a song was good Confucius would request for it to be repeated and then he would join in the singing. However, his thoughts about music also have something to do with social hierarchy. Confucius commented to the head of the Ji family that the *Boyi* dance and music should be played exclusively for the king of Zhou for "If he can bear to do this [listen to *Boyi* music], what may he not bear to do?" In this story, Confucius thought the head of the Ji family should not enjoy the music that only the king should enjoy. He considered it to be in contempt of the king.

Confucius said, "If a man is without the virtues proper to humanity, what has he to do with the rites of propriety? If a man be without the virtues proper to humanity, what has he to do with music?" He valued establishing rites and managing the country through propriety and music. The function of music was also mentioned in the *Analects of Confucius*: "The first to come observing ritual propriety and playing music were the simple folk; those who came later were the nobility. In putting ritual and music to use, I would follow those who came to them first."

Painting of Sage's Traces of the Ming Dynasty shows a scene where Confucius is being taught to play the *qin* by Shi Xiangzi. Confucius finally realizes the *qin* lyric that he is being taught is the *Exercise of Emperor Wenwang* composed by Emperor Wenwang of the Zhou Dynasty.

Confucian ideas about music had a conservative overtone. Confucius insisted on "being happy but not lascivious, and being sentimental but not mawkish." Music should be used to express moderate human feelings rather than excessive, animal-like emotions. He said music should be a sound of peace and harmony, that music should be in accordance with rites and not violate social etiquette, and should be a harmonious integration of beauty and kindness.

The Confucian philosopher Mencius considered music to be a natural way in which people expressed their thirst for happiness: loving beautiful music is human nature. Mencius also noted the educational role of music, pointing out that moral music was more influential than moral speeches. In his eyes, "sharing happiness with people" was the key in ancient times and modern days. This coincided with his belief that "the people were the most important element in a state; next were the gods of land and grain; least was the ruler himself." The ideas about music held by Confucius and Mencius are found only in isolated comments, but on their basis Confucians of later generations developed a relatively complex music ideological system.

Yuelun (*On Music*) written by Xunzi and *The Record of Music* that was finished in the Western Han Dynasty (206BC–25AD) summarized and developed early Confucian music ideas. *The Record of Music* held that music was something subjective affected by

Xunzi, a representative of the Confucianism, wrote *On Music*, a book about the general rules of music and its social functions.

objective matters, and that "only music could not be disguised, music is the revelation of one's true feelings." *Shangshu · Yaodian*, a classical work of the pre-Qin period, said music "was a link to the gods and ghosts and could inspire the dances of all beasts."

Xunzi Yuelun said, "Music could deeply touch the hearts of people and play its educational role quickly." Xunzi continued many Confucian ideas and developed them into the musical theory of the Legalist School. He believed that people needed music, but to stave off immorality and chaos, "The *Ya* and *Song* must be formulated to guide the development of music," and "efforts should be made to touch the good side of human nature and thus keep music from the evil spirits." Xunzi opposed "obscene music," "evil music" and "the music of Zheng and Wei Kingdoms," which actually referred to folk music. He said music "could educate people and deeply move them," and "transform outmoded habits and customs." The social function of music was thus elevated to a position of political education.

The *Dao* (natural way) of Heaven

Ancient Chinese philosophy included two concepts about "heaven": one was "the Dao (natural way) of heaven," which was to say, heaven was nature. As the Taoist philosopher Laozi said, "People should obey the earth, the earth obeys heaven, heaven obeys the Dao and Dao obeys nature" (*Tao Te Ching*). The relationship between humans and heaven was actually about relations between humans and nature. The other concept was that of "heaven's will," which held that heaven had its own will. Such famous words as "when former kings had any (important) business, they gave reverent heed to the commands of Heaven," suggest that heaven could be equal to the gods.

The Taoists pursued harmony between music and nature, and harmony between humans and the universe. They opposed shackling human nature and music, advocating music as a way to express people's true and natural feelings. The *Zhuangzi · qiwulun* says, "The sound of humans, earth and heaven" were the foundation of music. Here, the "sound of heaven" was that of nature, which reflected the view of music focusing on the "integration of humans and nature."

Dayin Xisheng or "a great music can not be heard" reflected Laozi's view towards music and a philosophical advance in the view of natural music at that time. Here, "great" might equal such Taoist concepts as "dao," "nature" and "inaction." The so-called "great music" referred to sounds in a natural state, and could be interpreted as the "sounds of heaven." *Dayin Xisheng* actually included two layers of meanings: i) The most beautiful music was that in line with the "dao"—the sound of heaven was natural and not man-made; ii) The nature of music was intangible and silent.

A statue of Laozi on Laojun Mountain, Quanzhou, Fujian Province.

Based on Laozi's theory of *Dayin Xisheng*, the philosopher Zhuangzi proposed a further series of concepts including: "The sound of heaven, earth, humans and natural happiness and ultimate happiness," "the heaven and earth show their beauty with no words," and "simplicity is beauty." These brought the ancient natural outlook on music to a higher philosophical level.

The core of Zhuangzi's view on music was the word *tian* (the heavens). "Heaven and earth show their beauty with no words," and the loudest and most beautiful music was the "sound of heaven," which coincided with the "integration of humans and heaven" that was advocated by Taoists. Zhuangzi dealt with the relationship between heaven and humans. Zhuangzi inherited Confucius's fatalistic inclination on this issue, abandoned the ideas that highlighted the positive action of people, denied the role of people in nature and further established his own ethical system. He believed humans came from nature, and all the

In the Dream with the Butterfly reflects Zhuangzi's philosophy.

creatures on the earth were from nature, but that humans could not change nature.

Most traditional Chinese artists have a deep affection for nature. Just as Ji Kang wrote in his *Eighteen Four-word Poems on His Brother's Entry into the Army*, "I feel free to use both my hands and eyes by playing the *qin* and looking up at the flying birds." Traditional Chinese music focused on expressions of people's feelings and experiences in nature and the integration of "humans and nature," which was closely associated with the influence of views advocated by Laozi and Zhuangzi. Undoubtedly, Zhuangzi was among the most important representatives of ancient China's outlook on music and nature.

The Inwardness of Zen

Zen is a school of Buddhism in China. Its doctrine focuses on an enlightened mind. Zen highlights introspection and sudden enlightenment, holding that for those who pursue Buddhism, the perfection of the self and becoming Buddha can be achieved so long as they enlighten their minds. In Zen beliefs the mind is very important for feeling music.

Zen upholds that one can hear "thunders in silence" by means of the force of one's mind, or by listening to the sound of a hand pressed against one's ear. Baiyin Master asked Buddhist monks to listen to the sound of a hand pressed against their ear. So long as one listens attentively, he or she can enter the spiritual realm. The music influenced by Zen pursues such Zen ideals as, "Everything is silent, only the sounds of bells can be heard."

Zen music and Confucian music share many characteristics, taking peace, simplicity, elegance and grandeur as their basic principle. Confucianism advocates music based on rituals, holding that music should serve rituals, and be subordinated to politics. The Zen masters also take music as a means to carry forward Buddhism. Zen upholds that if one can apprehend original nature, he or she can reach enlightenment. This kind of transcendent attitude towards life was suitable

Figures of Bodhidharma and His Six Successors in the collection of the Liaoning Provincial Museum portrays images of Bodhidharma, his second successor Divine Light, third successor Sengcan, fourth successor Daoshin, fifth successor Hongren and sixth successor Huineng.

Figure of the Eastern World Heavenly King named "Chiguo," god of music. Carrying a Chinese lute in his hands, he takes charge of converting all things to Buddhism through music.

for those ancient scholars who suffered from career setbacks and became disappointed in reality.

Ancient scholars pursued a peaceful mind, aiming for freedom of spirit and creation. These scholars promoted the development of traditional music, and freed it from the constraints of practical use, focusing instead on the thoughts and feelings of the creators.

A performance in Beijing's Zhi Hwa Temple of the ancient music derived from the imperial court music of the Tang and Dong dynasties. It is the only type of ancient music that was handed down from generation to generation. It was introduced to Zhi Hwa Temple at Lumichang Lane in Beijing in 1446 and has been passed down by monks.

Zen holds that musicians, in the creative process, should imagine themselves as the components of their works. This aims at shifting subjective thoughts and feelings into the music, or object, to reach two-way communication between the subject and the object. Zen calls the inwardness an assimilation of object and self. For the assimilation of object and self, or neglect of the boundary between object and self, the final goal is to reach a realm free from the constraints of the secular world. In short, Zen highlights the role of the mind, and music creation is not possible without the mind.

Ancient Confucianism, Taoism and Zen believed in the importance of harmony between man and nature, which has had a profound influence on China's traditional music. From this perspective, it is thought that the creation of music is based on mutual communication between objects and the self, and the exchange between the mind and objects. To have a true, detailed understanding of the enchantment of Chinese music, it is necessary to have a good understanding of the culture of ancient Chinese music.

Chapter 3
Chinese Musical Instruments

Chinese musical instruments are well known not only because of their long history, but also because of their great variety. According to records, more than twenty kinds of musical instruments emerged during the Yin and Shang dynasties, with percussion and wind instruments playing an important role. There were more than seventy different kinds of musical instruments used during the Zhou Dynasty, including percussion and wind instruments with fixed pitches. Until the early Qin period, musicians divided musical instruments into eight categories, known as the "eight instruments": gold, stone, earth, leather, silk, wood, gourd, and bamboo. From the Western Zhou Dynasty to the Spring and Autumn period, playing such musical instruments as the *sheng*, *yu* and *se* (wind instruments), the five-string lute, and qin zithers became popular in folk communities. During and after the Qin and Han dynasties, the *guzheng*, *pipa*, flute, *suona*, *huqin*, *ruan* (plucked string instruments), *yangqin* and other instruments also emerged. Some of these instruments were developed in China, while others were introduced from border ethnic groups or foreign states in the central plains of Asia.

Musical Instruments

Thanks to the efforts of many generations of musicians, China now has a large number of musical instruments. There are thought to be more than 600 varieties of Chinese musical instruments with unique characteristics. These traditional musical instruments can be divided into four general categories: wind, bowed, plucked strings and percussion.

Chinese wind instruments have a long and interesting history. Oracle-bone-scripts unearthed in the Yin Ruins show the names of wind instruments as the *he* (small *sheng*). Wind instruments make sounds through an air column, reed, or by coupling

Flutes.

A *yu* excavated from one of the tombs of the Western Han Dynasty at Mawangdui.

vibrations of both by airflow stimulation. Common wind instruments include the flute, *sheng*, *suona*, *xiao* (vertical bamboo flute), pipe, *bawu*, gourd flute and *lusheng* (reed-pipe).

Traditional flutes are made from bamboo. The flute has six tone holes, one blowing hole and one flute diaphragm hole. Ancient flutes were called *hengchui*. During the reign of Emperor Wudi of the Han Dynasty (156–87 BC), the flute was introduced to the Central Plains via the Western Regions. The flute tone limit can reach two and a half octaves. As the flute is small and easy to carry, with loud, clear timbre and rich expressive sound, it is often used for solos, ensembles, and accompaniments for operas, songs, and dances. It is a widely used and popular musical instrument.

The cross flute, also known as the G-tone flute, is used typically to accompany clapper opera drama in the north of China (clapper opera generally uses the G tone). The cross flute is thinner and shorter than the bamboo flute, boasting a clear and bright timbre. It is often used to express jubilant, lively and energetic feelings, and is chiefly associated with a strong northern style. Well-known flute songs like *Meet with Happiness*, *Five Bangzi* and *Birds in the Shade* are examples of works using the cross flute. The bamboo flute, also called D-tone flute, is an important instrument in Jiangnan string and wind music performances and Kunqu Opera. The bamboo flute is a little longer than the cross flute, with a beautiful timbre. It is often used to express delicate emotions, which are typical of the

Detail from *Tour on a Horse-drawn Carriage from the Ming Dynasty*. In front of the carriage is a band.

gentle Jiangnan style. Popular flute music includes *Journey to Suzhou*, *Flying Partridges* and *Zhonghua Liuban*.

The *sheng* is the earliest reed pipe wind instrument in China, and thought to be the world's first musical instrument to employ a free reed. It makes sounds through the combination of the reed, the pipe, and the free vibration of the reed in the reed frame. The *sheng* varies in shape and size, with long and short tubes, and consists of a hopper, bamboo pipe and reed. It is one of the most widely used instruments in the history of Chinese music and boasts a gentle timbre that suggests tranquility and peacefulness. It can be used to play not only monophony, but also harmony with outstanding effect, thus playing a prominent role in folk wind and percussion bands. It is also widely used as a singing accompaniment in folk arts, and as opera accompaniment.

Nowadays, the 17-reed *sheng* is more widely used. After the founding of the People's Republic of China in 1949, Chinese musical instrument makers and performers have made constant revisions to the *sheng*, and have developed the 21-reed *sheng*, 24-reed *sheng*, 36-reed *sheng*, 51-reed *sheng*, *kuoyin sheng*, *jiajian sheng*, mediant *sheng*, bass *sheng* and keyboard *pai sheng*.

The *suona* is found across the world in more than thirty countries in Asia, Africa and Europe. It emerged in China in about the third century AD. There is an image of a musician playing the *suona* on a fresco in the thirty-eighth cave of the Kizil Grottoes in Xinjiang's Baicheng. At present, the *suona* is popular in more than twenty ethnic groups in different regions of China, although its name varies from group to group. It is called *suona*, *laba*, *ji'na*, and *wulawa* by the Han; *sunaier* by Uyghurs; *bailai*, *zainai*, and *shala* by the Li people; and *bishikuer* and *narenbilige* by Mongolians. The *suona* generally consists of a double-reed whistle (made from reed), a core (made from copper), a rod (made

An elderly performer plays a *suona* by the Yellow River.

from white wood and rosewood) and a copper bowl (shaped like a loudspeaker). It sounds cheerful, loud, clear and harmonious. It is typically used as an accompanying musical instrument for wedding ceremonies, funerals and music festivals. One of the most famous pieces of music featuring the *suona* is *A Phoenix Worshipped by Hundreds of Birds*.

The *xiao*, also known as vertical flute, is a straight wind instrument. Different from the bamboo flute, it has fixed tone holes without a membrane hole. In ancient times, use of the *xiao* was spread among people living in Sichuan and Gansu. It is made of a bamboo pipe with a V-shaped mouthpiece. The *xiao* comes in a wide variety of different types, with common ones including

Painting of a Maid Playing a Xiao created by Tang Yin from the Ming Dynasty now in the Nanjing Museum collection.

the black bamboo *xiao*, the nine-section *xiao* and the *yuping xiao*. The *xiao* has a pure, soft and elegant sound, and is often used for playing long, peaceful and lyrical works. However, the volume is weak and it also has a very limited dynamic range. It is mostly used for solos or ensembles and is often accompanied by the *guqin* (*qin* zither), as can be heard in the song *Chun Jiang Hua Yue Ye*.

Bowed instruments are collectively called *huqin* in Chinese. Initially, the *huqin* were mainly used by people in the north. It was only during the Northern Song period (960–1126) that they were introduced to the central plains. After thousands of years of development by people of all ethnic groups, *huqin* have become an important part of Chinese musical instruments with strong characteristics. The *huqin* use a bow and strings to produce sound through friction, vibration and resonance. With rich, beautiful sound they are widely used for solos, ensembles and accompaniment. Nowadays, common bowed instruments include the *erhu*, *gaohu*, *zhonghu*, *jinghu* and horse-head stringed instruments.

The *erhu* is the most popular bowed instrument in China. It consists of a head, axis, rod, *qianjin*, *qinma*, sound box, strings and bow. Almost all of these parts are made from different types of wood, including red sandalwood, rosewood and ebony. The strings of the instrument are metal or metal over-spun strings. The strings of the bow are made from horsetail hairs. The *erhu* has a soft sound and is therefore best suited to playing soft, lyrical music. However, skillful *erhu* players can use it to play strong or cheerful melodies, and mimic the sounds of gongs and drums, horses and birdsong.

Thanks to the efforts of *erhu* performers in history, techniques of playing the *erhu* have witnessed great development over the centuries. Commonly used techniques include bow skills such as bow separation, fast bow, trembling bow, sudden bow and jump bow. Finger methods include rubbing, plucking, beating tone and sliding tone. For a long time, the *erhu* occupied a very important position in such musical

An *erhu*.

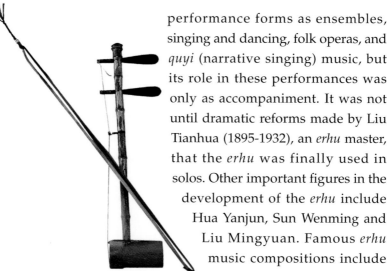

performance forms as ensembles, singing and dancing, folk operas, and *quyi* (narrative singing) music, but its role in these performances was only as accompaniment. It was not until dramatic reforms made by Liu Tianhua (1895-1932), an *erhu* master, that the *erhu* was finally used in solos. Other important figures in the development of the *erhu* include Hua Yanjun, Sun Wenming and Liu Mingyuan. Famous *erhu* music compositions include *The Moon Reflected on the Er-quan Spring*, *Listen to the Pine* and *Birds Singing on an Empty Mountain*.

A *jinghu* makes a loud and penetrating sound. It has been one of the main musical instruments used to accompany Peking Opera and *Hanju* Opera since the late Qing Dynasty.

The *banhu*, also called *yehu*, *qinhu*, *huhu*, *daxian* and *piao*, emerged at the same time as clapper opera. It is shorter than the *erhu*, and often made from coconut shells or wood and bamboo. The rods are mostly made from hard wood. The bow hair is placed between the two strings for playing. In the *huqin* family, the *banhu* is one of the powerful, high-tone instruments. Its timbre is sonorous and clear. It is often used to express lively, warm, and unrestrained feelings. The *banhu* is used for both solos and ensembles, and is also an important accompanying instrument for many different forms of opera, including the Hebei *bangzi*, *pingju* opera, *lü* opera, Henan Opera, Shaanxi Opera, Shanxi opera, Lanzhou drum opera and *daoqing* opera.

The horse-head string instrument is a unique bowed instrument of the Mongolian people. It is called *molin huer* by Mongolians. It is named after the horse's head carved on its upper part. Legend has it that the instrument became widespread among Mongolian people in the twelfth century. Its sound box is made from pine made into a trapezoidal shape. Both sides are covered with horse skin or sheepskin. Its rod is thin and long, made from elmwood or red sandalwood. The two strings are made from horsetail, as are the bowstrings. Capable of generating large volume and a mellow sound, it is often used for solos and as an accompaniment for folk songs and narrative singing.

Plucked string instruments are played using the fingers and/or bamboo to pluck the strings. They have an important place in the history of Chinese music. The *qin* and *se* emerged as early as the Zhou Dynasty. According to their shape, performance and playing methods, plucked string instruments can be divided into two broad categories: one represented by the *pipa*, and the other by the *guqin* and *guzheng*.

The *guqin* has been used in Chinese music for several thousand years. In 1977, the United States launched the spaceship Voyager to explore the outer reaches of the solar system. As it was the only man-made object ever to leave the solar system, it was decided that Voyager should carry information about human culture in case it should ever encounter alien life. A golden disc was made containing details about the scientific and cultural achievements of the human race. Twenty-seven pieces of music were selected for this purpose. *Flowing Water*, played on the *guqin*, was one of them. Since then, people around the world have paid attention to the ancient *guqin*. On November 7, 2003, the *guqin* was registered as an "Oral and Intangible Heritage of Humanity" by UNESCO.

The earliest *guqin* had five strings. Emperor Wenwang and Emperor Wuwang of the Zhou Dynasty in the eleventh century BC, both well educated in music, add two strings to the *guqin*. That is why the *guqin* usually has seven strings. The body of the *guqin* is usually elongated and hollow in the center. The seven strings hang above the surface of the *guqin* without supports. The surface of the *guqin* is used as the fingerplate. The surface board of the *guqin* is made of a whole piece of phoenix tree wood. Its surface is arched with two crescent- and square-shaped fixtures on the forehead and waist. There is huge variety in the ways in which the *guqin* can be played, with around ninety extant techniques.

The *guqin* has seven strings and is tuned to a pentatonic scale, with a major second or a minor third between adjoining strings. The ancient Chinese considered the *guqin* to be superior to all other instruments in depth and strength of musical expression. For example, according to Huan Tan's *New Discourses* the "qin is the best of all the stringed

Types of guqins
The *guqin* was first created in the Zhou Dynasty and then experienced a long evolution and development. The design was finalized in the Eastern Han Dynasy and Wei and Jin Periods. In accordance with *Wuzhi Zhai Qinpu* (a famous notation edited in the Qing Dynasty), the types of *guqin* include: *Fuxi, Shennong, Huangdi, Zhongni, Fengshi, Lingji, Lianzhu, Liezi, Shikuang, Shixiang, Boya, Luoxia, Jiaoye, Luqi, Ya'e, Jiaowei, Yushun, Yunhe, Hanqi, Longshou, Long'e, Longyao, Zhenghe, Qingying* and *Leiwei*. Out of them, *Fuxi, Shennong, Zhongni, Lianzhu, Luoxia* and *Jiaoye* are the most common types.

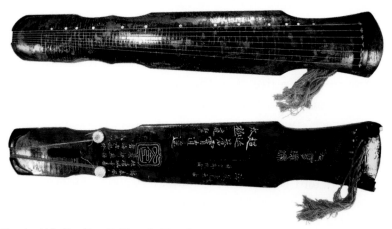

The *qin* of "*Jiu Xiao Huan Pei*" from the Tang Dynasty was designed in the *Fuxi* style. Its surface is made from a Paulownia tree in a semi-elliptical shape. Its body is made from Chinese fir and sculpted a round arris edge in the middle part and at the neck. The *qin* measures 124.5 cm long, making a chord length of 113 cm. It is 20.5 cm wide at the shoulder and 15.5 cm wide at the end, and 1.5 cm thick. It was originally painted black but was repainted chestnut brown at a later date. Above its "dragon pool" carvings are four Chinese characters "*Jiu Xiao Huan Pei*." It is now in the Palace Museum, Beijing.

Detail from *Painting of Listening to the Music of Qin* painted by Zhao Ji, Emperor Huizong of the Song Dynasty. The performer who sits under the pine tree is Zhao Ji himself.

instruments, which are the best of the eight kinds of musical instruments."

There are four traditional ways to play the *guqin*: solo, *qin* ensemble and *xiao* (a vertically-played bamboo flute), *qin* accompanying a song, and an ensemble of *gagaku* (a type of royal music from ancient China). Since ancient times, there have been thousands of solo pieces composed for the *guqin*. Some took natural scenes as their theme, such as *Lofty Mountains, Flowing Water, Three Variations of Plum Blossom* and *Wild Geese over the Clam Sands*. Some of them express the feelings and emotions of people, such as *Three Farewells at Yang Pass, Memory of an Old Friend, The Lament*, and *Misty Xiao Xiang River*. Other pieces are about historical and folk stories, such as *Song of the Autumn Frontier, The Song of Chu* and *Eighteen Songs of a Nomad Flute*.

Compared with other stringed instruments, such as the *guzheng*, the *guqin* is smaller with a thinner board. There is a thick layer of lacquer on the surface of the *guqin* and the sound it makes is softer than that played by the *guzheng*. The timbre of *guqin* is low and somewhat melancholy. It can sound firm and melodic, similar to the sound of musical bells and stones, or quiet and sweet, like the sound of a vertically played flute. The *guqin* is mainly used for self-entertainment as it is not really suitable for playing in front of many people. Zhuangzi once said, "By playing the *qin*, one can please himself." In essence, the *guqin* can be compared to a hermit who is introverted and thoughtful.

The *guqin* was popular among scholars, as they used it for the purpose of self-improvement. Before playing the *guqin*, the players would first wash their hands, tidy their clothes and burn some incense. They played the *guqin* not just for musical reasons, but also as a way of achieving harmony between human beings and nature. The ancients thought that to listen to music was akin to reading the feelings and intentions of a person. The *qin* was like a mirror which reflected the soul.

There are many stories about the *guqin*. One such story invloves Yu Boya and Zhong Ziqi. It is said that Yu Boya was good at playing the *guqin,* while Zhong Ziqi had a fine ear for *guqin* songs. Because of this, Zhong Ziqi knew what Yu Boya was thinking when playing his guqin. Once, Yu was thinking of lofty mountains when he was playing the *qin*, and Zhong said, "Fantastic, this music is as majestic as Taishan Mountain." Then Yu started to think of flowing water, and Zhong said, "Wonderful, the music flows as if running water." When Yu discovered that Zhong had died, he destroyed his *qin*, meaning he would never play the *guqin* again because he could not find anyone worthy of his performance. That is why the phrase *Gao Shan Liu Shui* (meaning the lofty mountain and flowing water) is now used as a metaphor for one's second self.

> **A *guqin* named "Raoliang"**
> There is a saying, *Yu Yin Rao Liang, San Ri Bu Jue*, meaning "the music ended long ago, but it still lingers in the mind" – this is the story behind it. It is said that the *quqin* named Raoliang was presented by Hua Yuan to King Zhuang of Chu, but no one knows when it was made. King Zhuang was very excited about receiving Raoliang. He played the *guqin* everyday, so much so, that he forgot to handle the affairs of his state for seven days. His wife, Fanji, was very worried and tried to persuade him to go back to work. She said, "In the past, Emperor Jie of the Xia Dynasty loved listening to music played by his wife Meixi so much that he lost his country, so did Emperor Zhou of the Shang Dynasty. Now, your Majesty, you love Raoliang so much. Do you want to lose your country?" After hearing her words, King Chu lost himself in meditation. Finally, he decided not to play the *guqin* any more, and let others destroy Raoliang with an iron tool.

Some people even found their lover when listening to *guqin* songs. Another story concerns Sima Xiangru and Zhuo Wenjun who lived in the Western Han Dynasty. Sima Xiangru was a famous poet and musician. He was good at playing the *qin*. The name of his *qin* was *lüqi*, one of the best *qin* in ancient China. When he was young, Sima Xiangru loved reading. Later in his life, Sima Xiangru fell on hard times and went to seek shelter with Wang Ji, a magistrate of Linqiong County. Wang Ji was friends with a rich man in the county called Zhuo Wangsun. He had a daughter named Zhuo Wenjun, who was then seventeen years old. She was a beautiful young woman and loved playing the drum and *qin*. In addition, she had a

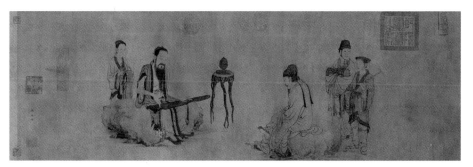

Painting of Yu Boya Playing the qin. The painting portrays Zhong Ziqi listening to the *qin* melody *Lofty Mountains and Flowing Water* played by Yu Boya.

natural talent for literature. At that time, her husband had just died. Sima Xiangru heard about Zhuo Wenjun and wanted to meet her. One day, he visited the Zhuo family and played a song on the *qin*, and sang:

> *This male phoenix has returned to his old home,*
> *From roaming the four seas searching for his mate;*
> *Time was not yet ripe; there was no way to meet her;*
> *Then what a surprise: this evening I come up to this hall,*
> *And there's a dazzling maiden in the women's quarters.*
> *The room is near but she is far: this poisons my guts.*
> *How can we entwine our necks like mandarin ducks?*
> *How can we flutter about, and together soar?*

A *guzheng.*

His direct, brave and passionate courtship moved Zhuo Wenjun, who had been listening to the song behind a curtain. They fell in love at first sight and then eloped. A piece of music based on this song of Sima Xiangru has been passed down for thousands of years and is called *A Male Phoenix Seeks his Mate*.

The *guzheng* is one of the oldest Chinese plucked string instruments. It became popular in the State of Qin (today's Shaanxi) as early as the Spring and Autumn Period (770-476 BC). During the Tang and Song dynasties, it had 13 strings, which later increased to 16, 18, 21 and 25 strings. The most commonly used *guzheng* has 21 strings. The sound quality depends on the quality of the panel and strings, and the four side-planks of the *guzheng* can be used to improve the timbre. The best timbers for the *guzheng* are old mahogany, red sandalwood, and golden-thread *nanmu*. It is played with the right hand playing the strings and the left hand adding pitch ornamentations and vibrato. There are many finger methods including holding, strumming, picking, wiping and shaking. The left hand performs actions such as pressing, sliding, kneading and trembling, and playing with sliding fingers to produce *glissando* (a slide from one pitch to another). It is often used for solos and ensembles, instrumental ensembles, as accompaniment for singing and dancing, operas and folk songs. With a broad tone range and beautiful timbre, it is known as the "King of Instruments," and the "Oriental Piano." Well-known *guzheng* compositions include *Song of the Homebound Fishermen* and *Lotus on Water*.

The second category of plucked string instrument in Chinese music is represented by the *pipa*, but also includes the *liuqin*, *yueqin*, *ruan* and *sanxian*. When it is played, the left hand controls the strings, and the right hand plays it. The *pipa* is an exotic musical instrument and was introduced to the Central Plains from India via Qiuzi (today's Kuqa in Xinjiang) during the Southern and Northern Dynasties. It is wooden with a

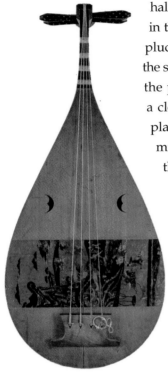

half-pear-shaped sound box. It is held vertically in the arms of the performer with the right hand plucking the strings and the left hand pinching the strings against the fret board in order to change the pitch. It has a broad range of sounds, with a clear and beautiful timbre. It can be used for playing impassioned performances of military music and lyrical cultural music. Along with the *guqin*, the *pipa* is considered to be one of the most important instruments in the history of music. Since the late Qing Dynasty, it has become an indispensable part of traditional Chinese musical culture. In addition to solo and orchestra performances, the *pipa* is widely used in opera, folk art and as accompaniment for singing. Well-known *pipa* compositions include *House of the Flying Daggers* and *Ambush on Ten Sides*.

Percussion instruments are the oldest known instruments in human history. Sounds are made by striking the body of the instrument. Common percussion instruments include the clapper drum, waist drum, wood block, small gong, big gong, *yunluo*, cymbal and the hand bell. In addition, the *yangqin* is also classified as a percussion instrument. All ethnic groups have different styles of drums. Commonly used drums in South East Asia include the hand drum of the Uygur people, the *bajiao* drum (eight-angled drum) of the Manchu and Bai people, the elephant-foot drum of the Dai people, the long drum of the Yao people, the hand drum of the Tibetans and the hourglass-shaped drum of ethnic Koreans.

A Chinese *pipa*, which is part of a collection in Shosoin, Japan.

The *yangqin*, which is also known as a dulcimer, was first introduced to China from Persia (today's Iran) and Arabia towards the end of the Ming Dynasty. It was first popular in Guangdong, and later all over the country. It is made of wood, with the main framework functioning as its resonance box. This framework is often in the shape of a butterfly; hence it is sometimes called the "butterfly dulcimer." When played, it is placed on a wooden stand with both hands holding small, flexible bamboo sticks that are used to strike the strings. It boasts bright and clear sounds suitable for the performance of light, lively and cheerful music. It can be used for solos, ensembles, *quyi* music and opera accompaniment. It has experienced many years of development and is one of the most popular musical instruments in China.

Drums are made from wood with a round framework covered with animal skin. They come in many different shapes and sizes. Big drums are played using two thick wooden sticks, making different sounds with different pitches and timbre depending on where it is struck. The center of the drum makes downbeat sounds with the sound becoming increasingly strong as one moves from the center to the edge. Big drums tend to be used for drum and gong bands or national music bands to create an atmosphere. The *bangu* (clapper drum) is covered with a single layer of animal skin. With a thick frame and small drum heart, thin bamboo sticks are used to strike the drum heart to make high-pitched sounds. These are generally used as an accompaniment for Peking Opera and other local operas.

The gong is made from copper. Round with low sounds in the center and high-pitched sounds on the edges, the big gong boasts a rough and loud timbre. It is often used in national instrumental ensembles. The *yunluo* (Chinese gong chimes) is an instrument with fixed pitches that can play melodies. It consists of a number of small brass gongs that are arranged on a wooden stand according to their order of pitch. The number of gong chimes on

This waist drum is a cylindrical-shaped percussion instrument that is wide in the middle and narrow at both ends. It is used to accompany waist drum dances or folk songs and dances.

each *yunluo* varies. The playing method is similar to that of the dulcimer, including clicking, double-clicking, rolling striking, light striking and heavy striking. It can also play double tones, arpeggios and tetrameter chords (both hands holding two sticks striking at the same time). The *yunluo* boasts a clear and bright timbre, and can also be used for accompaniment, ensembles and for solos.

Varieties of Unique Local Music

China's instrumental music can be divided into two major categories: solo and ensemble. There are numerous pieces of solo composition, and ensemble pieces, including Guangdong music, Jiangnan string and woodwind instrumental music, Chaozhou string music, Xi'an drum music, and Jiangsu *shifangu* (ten drum sound variations), totaling more than 10,000 compositions. These are important components of traditional Chinese music. Based on the characteristics of various local music and orchestral

A wood-block New Year painting of "Shi Bu Xian" from Yangliuqing, Tianjin: "Shi Bu Xian" is mostly performed at fairs. In the performance, one performer plays the main role while others accompany him with musical instruments.

formulation and performance, they can be divided into five categories: string and woodwind instrumental music, string music, wind and drum music, wind and percussion music, and drum and gong music.

String and woodwind instrumental music involves one or two string instruments and bamboo wind instruments performing as an ensemble. This kind of music is popular mainly in the south and is noted for its refinement and elegance. Jiangnan string and wind instrumental music, Guangdong music and Fujian Nanyin music are all important examples of this type of music. Jiangnan string and wind music is a kind of string and wind instrumental ensemble music popular in Shanghai, Jiangsu and Zhejiang in modern China. Wenming Yaji is a kind of string and wind instrumental music established in Shanghai in 1911. Performed on a regular basis, famous pieces included *Er Liu*, *On the Street*, and *Song of Joy*. Later, the Jun Tian Music Society, Society of National Music, Shanghai Traditional Music Research Association, and other such groups were established, playing a positive role in driving the development of Jiangnan string and wind instrumental music. The main instruments used include the flute, *erhu*, *sanxian*, *pipa*, dulcimer, vertical flute, *sheng*, drum, clappers and wood block. Famous music pieces associated with this genre are generally known as the "eight pieces," namely *Lao Sanliu*, *Man Sanliu*, *Zhonghua Liuban*, *Man Liuban*, *Song of Joy*, *Yunqing*, *Si He Ru Yi* and *On the Street*.

Guangdong music consists of string and wind instrumental ensemble music that originated from Guangzhou and the Pearl River Delta region in the late nineteenth century. When it first emerged, this kind of music focused on the performance of songs, *qupai* music and interlude music in local opera. Often used for folk customs and festivals, it later evolved into instrumental music with Guangdong characteristics. Well-known performers included Yan Laolie, Qiu Hechuan, Lu Yicheng and He Liutang

A performance by the Quanzhou Nanyin Ensemble, Fujian Province.

who, in addition to performance, adaptation, and general development of musical instruments, also wrote many musical compositions. Guangdong music was usually performed in an ensemble of five-stringed instruments played with a high tension bow or by an ensemble of three low bow tension instruments. At the present time, the main musical instruments employed in Guangdong music are the *gaohu* (Cantonese *huqin*), *yangqin*, *pipa*, vertical flute, *yehu* and *guzheng*. Famous compositions include *Zao Tian Lei, Descending Curtain, Chain of Rings, Rain Pattering on Plantain Leaves, Peach Blossom, Bitter Hate, Climbing High Step-by-step* and *Autumn Moon Over the Calm Lake*.

Fujian Nanyin music has a long and distinguished history. Frescos dating back to the Tang Dynasty clearly show musical performances using the Nanyin pipa, vertical flute and clappers. This is clear evidence that something like Fujian Nanyin music was popular at that time. Further evidence is provided by the fact that song titles of modern Nanyin music are closely related to those of the Tang Dynasty. Fujian Nanyin music was widespread in Fujian during the Qing Dynasty, and is now popular in some countries in Southeast Asia.

The performance forms of Fujian Nanyin fall into two categories: *shangsiguan* and *xiasiguan*. The instruments included in the *shangsiguan* are the vertical flute, *erxian*, *pipa*, *sanxian* and clappers, mainly played indoors. The instruments included in the *xiasiguan* include mediant *suona*, *pipa*, *sanxian*, *erxian* and some small percussion instruments, which are mostly played outdoors. Nanyin consists of three components, namely, *zhi*, *pu* and *qu*. *Zhi* includes large-scale suite music. Each set of *zhi* music includes a *libretto*, score and *pipa* performance with a narrative. *Pu* means suites of instrumental music, so they are instrumental divertimento music. For instrumental *divertimento* music, each *divertimento* includes a *gong-chi* music score and *pipa* performance. The most widespread ones focus on the description of natural landscapes, flowers, birds and insects. Representative works include *Four Seasons, Plums, Eight Galloping Horses* and *Birds Returning to Their Nests. Qu* refers to *sanqu*, and is an independent form of vocal *music*. Representative pieces include *Dagun, Zhong Gun, Da Bei* and *Zhong Bei*.

Chinese traditional string music, also known as string music, Xuanshi music, or *xiyue* (fine music), is popular in the north, south and central plains. It was used to accompany operas and folk arts in the Song and Yuan dynasties. Later, it referred to music ensembles featuring several plucked stringed instruments and bowed instruments. Because of its elegant style and long history, Chinese traditional string music is also known as elegant and ancient music, with typical examples including the ensemble of thirteen stringed musical instruments of Beijing, the *bantou* tunes of Henan and the fine music of Chaozhou. Despite variations in local features and styles, these different forms of traditional string music have a lot in common, including band composition, performance style and the structure of the music. Generally, only three or four instruments with local characteristics are used, such as the *guzheng, pipa, yangqin, sanxian* and *huqin*.

Wind and drum music involves instruments such as pipes, *suona, haidi* (smaller-sized *suona*), and flutes, along with other orchestral and percussion instruments. There are wide varieties of wind and drum music throughout China. They can be divided into three categories: wind and drum music based mainly on pipes, with representatives including the Hebei Music Association, North Shanxi folk pipe-wind music and music of the Beijing Zhihua Temple; wind and drum music based mainly on the *suona* (or *haidi*), with representatives including wind and drum music of Jilin, Liaoning, east Hebei, southwest Shandong, Shanxi and Yili; and wind and drum music based mainly on the flute, from southwest and central Shandong.

"Twelve Fashionable Girls", a popular new folk band.

Wind and percussion ensemble features orchestral instruments or wind and percussion instruments. Wind and percussion ensembles are popular mainly in the southern part of China. Well-known examples of this type of music include the South Jiangsu *shifangu*, the *shifan* drums and gongs, and the wind and percussion ensemble of Zhejiang. Xi'an drum music, popular in Xi'an and its neighboring regions, is also a kind of large-scale wind and percussion ensemble with a long history. According to recent research, it originated from *yanyue* (court banquet music) of the Tang Dynasty. It is imperial music characterized by grandness, graciousness, elegance, rich compositions and structural integrity. Its structure is similar to that of grand pieces from the Tang Dynasty. Xi'an drum music is mainly based on bamboo flutes and comes in two different forms depending on whether it is played inside or outdoors. The outdoor form of Xi'an drum music is played in the streets at temple fairs and on other occasions.

Chapter 4
Chinese Folk Songs

China's vast territory, complicated topography and climate, and different folk customs have combined to create a rich variety of folk songs. Chinese folk songs have had a crucial role to play in the development of Chinese musical culture. They have had an important influence on the development of a number of different art forms, including singing, dancing, *quyi* and opera. As early as the pre-Qin period, the ancient Han people developed a rich and varied folk music tradition. In the Han Dynasty, a national musical institution called *yuefu* was set up by the government, which was responsible for collecting folk songs and compiling them into *yuefu* poems. Folk songs in the Han Dynasty were classified into *tuge* (solo singing without music), *dange* (duet), and *xianghege* (responsive singing). From the Northern Wei to the Sui and Tang dynasties, folk Han music in southern and northern China were collectively called *qingshangyue* or *qingyue*. It included folk songs and dancing music, and also formed part of the *yanyue* "banquet music." In the Tang Dynasty, folk songs were called *quzi*. In relics unearthed from the Cangjing Cave at Dunhuang, as many as 590 *quzici* songs were discovered, involving more than 80 kinds of melodies. In the Song and Yuan dynasties, *zaju* (variety play) music and southern opera music became the main form of music, which also absorbed a lot of musical elements from folk songs. *Zaju* music was formed by absorbing *gewudaqu* (singing and dancing performance), northern narrative-singing music and folk tunes. Southern opera music included folk tunes and songs that were popular in the south, the popular *cidiao* (tonal patterns) and the music of *gewudaqu*.

Han folk songs have short structures, flexible rhythms, concise and simple melodies, and employ vivid musical imagery. The reason why Han folk songs became such an important influence on the music of later centuries is that they originated from the life of the working people. These songs were an important part of their culture and were passed down from generation to generation. Because this transmission was largely oral, this led to interesting variations and developments in folk songs over the passage of time. The folk songs of the Han Chinese can be classified into three basic types—*haozi* labor songs, mountain songs and folk tunes.

Haozi Labor Songs

Haozi is a form of folk song strongly associated with manual labor. It evolved from the shouts naturally uttered while working. Aside from any artistic functions, it performs a variety of more utilitarian functions such as providing directions for particular tasks, team building and general encouragement. It uses a basic form of call and response, or "one singing responded by many," and reflects the toughness and strength of physical labor through affirmative, sometimes even heroic, melodies and rhythm. Generally speaking, the more strenuous the labor is, the shorter the rhythm, and the simpler the melody.

Laborers sing *Haozi* while working..

There is a large variety of traditional *haozi*, which are classified according to the type of labor with which they are associated. Examples include porting *haozi*, engineering *haozi*, agricultural *haozi*, workshop *haozi* and fishing boat *haozi*. "Porters don't mind bending *biandan* (a carrying pole)" is a porting *haozi* that is popular in northern Jiangsu Province. When transporting cargo with carrying poles on their shoulders, the porters sing this *haozi* to a short and even rhythm to keep energized and, more importantly, to keep in step with each other. *Da Hang Ge* (*Ramming Song*) is an engineering *haozi* sung while building dams and roads. A *hang* is a stone rammer comprised of a heavy stone or round log hung under two parallel wooden rods (or four rods in the shape of a hash character "#") and is lifted up by two or four

Boatmen sing *Haozi* by the Yellow River.

people then pushed down with great force. Different places had different *Da Hang Ge* with different melodies, but they are all based on a strong underlying rhythm.

Fishing boat *haozi* were sung when boating and fishing in rivers, lakes and seas. Because of its complex working conditions and the intensity of labor involved, the music of fishing boat *haozi* is perhaps the most rich and abundant of all the *haozi*. A quintessential example of this type of *haozi* is *Boating Haozi on the Chuanjiang River*. The natural conditions of the Chuanjiang River are complex, as the river winds along many sandbanks causing the water sometimes to flow quickly and at other times slowly. The *haozi* sung by the boatmen when floating on the Chuanjiang River varies according to which part of the river they are navigating and the river conditions at that particular time. Thus it is comprised of eight different passages of *haozi*, including *Pingshui haozi* (flat water *haozi*), *Jiantan haozi* (shoal-seeing *haozi*), *Shangtan haozi* (going up the sandbank *haozi*), *Xiatan haozi* (going down the sandbank *haozi*), and so on. *Pingshui haozi* is sung when the water is still and the boat has just started its voyage. It is melodious with a stable rhythm. *Jiantan haozi* is sung by the lead singer on the boat when passing by a dangerous sandbank to warn his fellow boatmen. Therefore its rhythm is tight and compact, using very short sentences, reflecting the tense atmosphere. The whole song of *Boating Haozi on the Chuanjiang River* is rich in changes of mood and dynamics, reflecting the different conditions the boatmen face on their journey.

Mountain Songs

Mountain songs are inspired by a love of nature and the wilderness. The rhythms of mountain songs are free, the tunes sonorous, loud and clear, and the lyrics are often associated with the natural scenery. They begin with phrases like "The sun

A folk singer from northern Shaanxi Province sings a freestyle song of *Xin Tian You*.

rises…," "The moon rises…," "The river floods…," "On the high mountain…," and so on.

Mountain songs vary greatly depending on differences in local culture and dialect. With the Yangtze River as a natural border, the mountain songs of the north have special names. The mountain songs in northern Shaanxi are called *Xin Tian You*, in the regions of Qinghai, Ningxia, and Gansu they are *huaer*, in Inner Mongolia *pashan diao*, and in Shanxi they are called *shan qu*. In southern China, mountain songs are named after places, such as the Jiangzhe mountain songs, Kejia mountain songs, Xiang E mountain songs, Southwest mountain songs, and Tianyang mountain songs.

The subjects covered by mountain songs are diverse, involving many different aspects of life. *Xin Tian You* talks about the natural landscape of the Loess Plateau in the northwest and the bold unrestrained spirits of northwestern people, while *Fishing Songs* reflects the laboring life in the region south of the Yangtze River.

The *huaer* song *Going down to Sichuan* is about the *jiaohuge*, the peasants living by transporting goods with mules in the poor mountainous regions in northwest China. It paints a vivid picture of peasants leaving their hometowns with their livestock to seek a living in Sichuan. The melody is soft and undulating, and the rhythm is stretching, sad and touching. It conveys a mood of melancholy and homesickness.

The plain mountain songs are a favorite of people in many parts of China. In the northwest of Shanxi, north of Shaanxi and the western part of Inner Mongolia, every person—man, woman, elder or child—can sing mountain songs. Their tunes are sonorous, loud and clear, their vocal range broad, and their rhythm free. Some short pieces of mountain songs will often vary according to the different moods and experiences of the singers. In Shanxi Province, the most famous place for mountain songs is in Hequ. This small place, with the large winding Yellow River passing through the northwest part of Shanxi, has given birth to a most popular Shanxi folk song called *Zou Xikou* (*Walking through the West Port*). At the end of the Qing Dynasty and the beginning of the Republic of China in 1911, the regions along Hequ and Baode experienced natural disasters and famine. The peasants were forced to migrate through the port of the ancient Great Wall on the border of Shanxi and Inner Mongolia (Xikou) to avoid famine and eke out a living, which was called *Zou Xikou*. The folk song *Zou Xikou* reflects the pain of these people having to leave their loved ones at this time.

Folk Songs

"What a beautiful jasmine flower..."

These words are from *Jasmine Flower*, one of the most famous folk songs in Chinese music. According to Qian Renkang, an expert on Chinese music, it was the first Chinese folk song to become popular and well known outside China. The song tells the story of a girl who wants to pick a beautiful jasmine flower but who fears the criticism of the person guarding the flower. Such is the importance of this song in Chinese culture, it was chosen as the song to accompany the medal ceremonies at the 2008 Beijing Olympic Games.

Jasmine Flower is a quintessential folk ditty of the Han Chinese. A ditty is another form of folk song of the Han. All small folk songs sung in daily life are called ditties. The melody of ditties is beautiful and smooth, with a regular, structured rhythm. The content of such songs is often expressed in an indirect way, with feelings attributed to the landscape or emotions being expressed through legends. Sometimes string accompaniments are added, making the music of ditties much more beautiful and touching.

There is a rich variety of folk ditties. They can be classified into three basic types according to their historical origin, the occasion for singing them and their musical character. The first type are

Fresh and elegant jasmine flowers.

Xiu Hebao
The original name of *Xiu Hebao* is *Huguang Diao*, originally from the region of Hunan and Canton in south China. It has been a popular ditty since the Ming and Qing dynasties. It was named *Xiu Hebao* because it used a melody to accompany the lyrics of *Embroidering Hebao*. *Hebao* (purse) is a souvenir signifying the love between a Chinese man and woman and their acceptance of each other. Folk songs about embroidering *hebao* are sung all over China with a rich variety of melodies. *Xiu Hebao* in Shanxi, Yunnan, and Sichuan are the most familiar. They depict the thoughts of young girls missing their lovers and personally embroidering *hebao* for their beloved.

folk songs from the Ming and Qing dynasties, such as *Nao Wujing, Shua Haier, Yin Niusi* and *Die Duanqiao*—all from the Ming Dynasty; and *Jian Dinghua, Yu E Lang, Xianhua Diao*, and *Huguang Diao* (*Xiu Hebao*)—all from the Qing Dynasty. Some have retained their original title, whereas some have kept almost the same melody but the name has been changed. For example, the melody of *Jian Dinghua* is used in many pieces across the country such as *Fang Fengzheng, Diu Jiezhi, Siji Ge*, and *Xiu Wujing*. In total, there are ten known variations of this melody.

The second type of folk ditty is sung impromptu. These types of folk ditty are pure, simple and plain, with strong regional characteristics. A typical example of this is *Cai Diao* in the Yunnan Province, which is often sung by children playing when playing games. The third type of folk ditty is used for singing and

Two girls sing the Chinese folk song *Jasmine Flower*.

dancing at folk festivals in a variety of different regions. They feature distinct jumping rhythms and smooth melodies. Examples of this include *Huagu Diao, Deng Diao, Huadeng Diao, Caicha Diao* in south China and *Yang Ge Diao* in north China, as well as *Pao Hanchuan* that were popular nationwide. The most famous are *Fengyang Huagu*, a Huagu *diao* of Anhui, *Shi Dajie*, a Caicha *diao* of Yunnan and *Pao Hanchuan* sung in the northern part of Shaanxi.

During the passage of time, folk songs were passed down from generation to generation and, in the process, were often altered by professional and semi-professional folk artists. This process of gradual change has led to the development of many different variants across China. For example, after *Jasmine Flower* spread to different regions, many variations appeared, both north and south of the Yangtze River. In 1804, John Barrow, part of the first British embassy to China, recorded in his *Travels in China* that "*Jasmine Flower* seems to be one of the most popular songs in China." Moreover, *Jasmine Flower* also spread abroad through the development exchange of Sino-foreign relations. Well-known musicians of different countries appropriated the melodies of *Jasmine Flower* for their own purposes. For example, Italian composer Giacomo Puccini used the melody of *Jasmine Flower* in his opera *Turandot*. More recently, Kenny G, a well-known American saxophone player, adapted and performed *Jasmine Flower* for American audiences. In 1982, UNESCO compiled a list of recommended songs from around the world and *Jasmine Flower* was among them.

The different ecological environments of China have created folk songs of different styles. The

Meng-Jiang Nü
Meng-Jiang Nü is the earliest folk ditty known throughout in China. The song originated from the widely spread legend of *Meng-Jiang Nü Wailing at the Great Wall*, telling a sad story about a newlywed couple being separated. *Meng-Jiang Nü* of Jiangsu is one of the original forms. Its delicate melody is quintessentially Jiangnan style. After spreading to different places, many variations appeared in different places with different customs.

Jasmine Flower, a famous Chinese folk song, was adopted by Italian composer Giacomo Puccini in *Turandot*, a famous opera based on a Chinese story.

mountain songs in the western mountains and the plateau region are resounding and passionate, while the ditties in the eastern plains are fresh, smooth and delicate. Over the course of time, the cultural connotations of folk songs have gone far beyond the songs themselves. They reflect the ancient oral culture of China and have become a store of cultural heritage that can be shared with the rest of the world.

Chapter 5
The Singing and Dancing
of Ethnic Groups

China consists of fifty-six different ethnic groups. The Han Chinese are the largest ethnic group in China, constituting about 92% of the population. Because of their relative size, the other fifty-five ethnic groups are known as minorities. People of all ethnic groups are known for their singing and dancing accompanied by distinct varieties of folk music. Just like the Han, all of the ethnic groups in China have created their own folk songs and dances such as *Flower*, a song of the Hui people; *long tone* and *Hoomei* songs of the Mongolians; special types of music like *muqam* of the Uygurs; the *dongjing* music of the Naxi people; folk dances like long-dram dance of the ethnic Korean people; timbal dance and tap dance of the Miao, Yao and Yi peoples; the *andai* dance of the Mongolians; the *caicha* dance of the Zhuang people. Chinese ethnic groups are also responsible for developing a number of distinct operatic traditions, including folk operas such as Tibetan Opera, the *Baiju* Opera of the Bai people and *Zhuangju* Opera of the Zhuang people. These songs, dances and operas make up the brilliant musical culture of China and have an important place in Chinese music history.

Muqam of the Uygur People

The Uygur minority inhabits the Xinjiang Uygur Autonomous Region in the northwestern part of China. The Uygurs enjoy singing and dancing, both in festivals and as part of their leisure activities. In fact, singing and dancing are important parts of their lives, as they consider them to be a crucial way of expressing their emotions. The Uygyurs are quoted as saying: "We are frequently sing and dance in our lives just like people of other ethnic groups must put salt in their meals. We can sing and dance anywhere, anytime." The graceful Uygur songs and dances have found popularity

Muqam is reputed to be the mother of Uygur music.

around the world, especially *muqam*, a type of traditional Uygur music that is known for its abundant content, colorful melodies and diverse musical structures. It can be traced as far back as 1500 BC and flourished until 1600.

Based on region and stylistic features, *muqam* can be divided into four basic types: Nanjiang *muqam*, Beijiang *muqam*, Dongjiang *muqam*, and Doran *muqam* from the Tarim Basin. Of these, the Nanjing *muqam* is perhaps the most interesting. It consists of twelve sets of songs, dances and music, and hence it is known as the "Twelve *Muqam*." Each set is performed for about two hours and is made up of four parts: *Muqam*, a lyric free rhythm; *Qong Nagma*, a collection of seven or eight songs connected by interludes; *Dastan*, three to five lyric ballads of different beats and tempos in a whole structure; and *Mashirapu*, a "cheerful evening party" composed of three to six dances and songs of different tempos, vivid melodies and lively tones. Accompanied by the *sataer, tanboer, dutaer, rewapu, aijieka, qalun* and hand drum, the "Twelve *muqam*" are usually performed by a group of people. At the beginning, they all sit together and one of the performers begins a solo, followed by several performers on the hand drums. Then all the dancers, men and women, begin to dance in pairs. With a fast tempo, they change their dance movements periodically until the music reaches a climax. Because *muqam* is easily performed, it has become popular with the general public. In 2005, the United Nations Educational Scientific and Cultural Organization (UNESCO) enlisted *muqam* into the third batch of masterpieces of the Oral and Intangible Heritage of Humanity.

Tibetan Folk Songs and Dances

Tibet is mountainous country on the northern side of the Himalayas. It is the highest region in the world and so is popularly known as the "roof of the world." The Tibetan people celebrate all aspects of life and work in their songs. They glorify the mountains and rivers, praise labor and admire the love between men and women. Tibetan folk songs include the following: songs for children, toasting, working, pastoral songs and mountain songs.

Of these, toasting songs are a favorite among Tibetans. This type of song features a fresh and smooth melody and is usually sung to propose a toast at social gatherings. On the occasions of traditional festivals, parties or wedding ceremonies, people sit around a Tibetan-type square table in

The singing of Tibetans wafts over the snowy mountains.

order of seniority in the family. One of them, usually a woman, acts as the cupbearer. She has to fill every cup while singing and dancing. After they are served, each drinker is supposed to receive a cup, point to heaven with the ring finger, take three sips and finish the drink in a special posture as required in the song.

Duixie or *duidi* song and dance is another important part of Tibetan culture. *Duidi* refers to the area of the upper reaches of the Brahmaputra River and the Ali Prefecture. Tibetans call the area *dui* and name the dance which comes from the area *duixie*. *Duixie* songs are distinct, vivid and lively; while *duixie* dances are performed in warm and flexible movements. In form, *duixie* is made up of *jiangxie* and *juexie*. *Jiangxie* is comprised of songs with a slow tempo and melodious tones, while *juexie* are dances with a fast tempo and vigorous movements. *Duixie* is usually accompanied by *terz* guitars and the performance of a tap dancer. The tap dancer makes sounds with complicated movements of the feet such as kicking, tapping, stamping and jumping. *Duixie* is performed either in festivals or during leisure time. It can be performed in many different ways, whether in costume or not. It is becoming more and more popular with folk artists and the Tibetan people.

Tibetan songs and dances.

Nangma is another traditional type of song and dance of the Tibetan people. Accompanied by the bamboo flute, *yangqin*, *gengka*, *urheen*, *chiqin* and tinkle bells, performers usually set the tone according to the main musical instrument first, followed by singing in a lyrical and graceful melody and dancing at a fast tempo. In recent years, *nangma* has become popular in Lhasa, the capital of Tibet. Today, people like to attend authentic performances of *nangma*, sometimes even taking part in dances themselves.

Mongolian Folk Songs

The Mongolians who inhabit the vast plain in the northern part of China have been called the "ethnic group of music and poems." The people have created a large quantity of folk songs, which are all performed in a characteristic way. As a Mongolian saying goes in the Hetao Region of Inner Mongolia, "Folk songs are as plentiful as blackberries in Hetao, one could sing only a small number of them in three years."

Mongolian folk songs are divided into several different types, such as pastoral, ballads, folk, dinner, wedding, working and hunting. The well-known *Gada Meilin* is a lengthy ballad. Based on musical features, there are two types of Mongolian folk songs performed: long tone and short tone. The long tone is characterized by a falling and rising melody with a free rhythm. Praise songs, pastoral songs and some folk songs are long tone, and they are usually sung at a party, wedding or *Maadam*. In contrast, the short tone is marked by a relaxed and cheerful melody, a tight structure and a short length. Hunting songs, ballads and some folk dances fall into this category.

Khuumei is a special kind of throat singing where one performer can sing two voice parts, a unique talent of the Mongolian people. It is said that the ancestors of the Mongolians

Mongolian songs express a bold and unrestrained melody.

created *khuumei* by imitating the sounds of running streams and waterfalls echoed in the mountains. The performer sings the raucous base part by holding their breath and then impacting his vocal cord with breaths. He then makes a clear melodic treble voice by creating a resonance inside the oral cavity, intensifying and concentrating overtones, so as to produce a wonderful and hypnotic sound effect.

Dong's *Ka Lau*

The Dong people inhabit the Guizhou, Hunan and Guangxi provinces of China. They are a very creative people. As the saying goes, "Dong's culture is composed of three treasures: the Drum Tower, *Ka Lau* and flower bridges." Of them, the Drum Tower and flower bridges are famous constructions, whereas *Ka Lau* is a form of folk music. The Dong people refer to *Ka Lau* as *Kgal Laox*. "*Kgal*" refers to songs, while "*Laox*" means grand and ancient. *Ka Lau* is a unique multi-part, *a cappela* form of choral singing in which one performer leads the chorus, while the other three to five singers form a male or female voice part. Its main theme is sung by the base section with the treble part being provided by a smaller group of performers, at most three singers.

Ka Lau features rhymed lyrics and graceful tones. Its lyrics, composed usually by means of comparison and metaphor, celebrate nature, labor work, love and friendship. *Ka Lau* makes use of sounds found in nature. For example, the songs are often enhanced with the sounds of bird chirping and babbling brooks. Performances of *Ka Lau* are often presented in that other symbol of Dong culture, the Drum Tower, and also at local festivals and events.

All *Ka Lau* performers have an accurate command of absolute pitch. In a chorus, all of them sound the intonation of the same tone. They can do this because they have had strict training since childhood. Their parents teach them children's songs at an early

The Drum Tower is a landmark of the Dong village and stage for *Ka Lau*.

Two Dong women enjoy local music and song. The native land of the ethnic Dong people is honored as the "Ocean of Songs."

age and send them to a folk-song master at about ten years of age. Although the master teaches them free of charge, they must perform a series of rigorous exercises. They learn lyrics and musical notation in different singing groups according to their gender and age. On that basis, the master selects singers according to their vocal ability and gives them additional lessons.

Miao's Folk Songs and Musical Instruments

The Miao people inhabit Guizhou, Yunnan, Hunan, Sichuan, Guangxi, Hubei and Guangdong provinces in southern China.

A Miao man playing a *lusheng*.

The Miao minority is said to have originated from the *Jiuli*, a tribe that inhabited the middle and lower reaches of the Yellow River 5,000 years ago. Later they moved to the middle and lower reaches of the Yangtze River and formed the Sanmiao tribe. Through the passage of time, Miao people migrated all over the southern part of China and have crossed borders to other countries. Today, Miao people can be found in Vietnam, Thailand, Laos, Europe and America. Similar to other ethnic groups, Miao people enjoy singing and dancing, especially in festivals.

There is a great variety of Miao folk songs. As for content, they contain hundreds of varieties; their love songs alone can be divided into thirteen types, such as songs about encounters, couples in love and courtship. In terms of literary form, these folk songs can be divided into long tones and short tones. The long tone consists of narrative epics and ballads told in a primitive and bold manner. The short tone covers all folk songs apart from epics and ballads, such as work songs, canzonets, songs for customs and children's songs.

The Fly Tone, a type of Miao folk song, is popular in Taijiang, Jianhe and Kaili, Guizhou. Since this type of song is presented in a loud and sonorous tone, singers have to sing in falsetto. The lyrics involve words of admiration, appreciation and encouragement. In celebrating the Miao New Year or Dragon Boat Festival, Miao people always sing Fly Tones to show their happiness.

Miao folk musical instruments can be summed up as "three drums and one *sheng*." The "three drums" refer to the bronze, wooden and leather drums; while the "one *sheng*" is *lusheng* (a reed wind instrument). The *lusheng* comes in many different sizes. The small-sized treble *lusheng* is a mere 33 cm long, whereas the big-base *lusheng* can be as long as 330 cm. They are often used in groups but can also be used as solo accompaniment for dances.

Accompanied by the bronze drum, wooden drum and *lusheng*, Miao dances are named after musical instruments, such as the Bronze Drum Dance, the Wooden Drum Dance and the *Lusheng* Dance. Of these, the *Lusheng* Dance is the most popular. It is performed with active movements like squatting, jumping and marching. It is well known for the difficulty of these movements. For example, at one point in the dance, performers are required to do a squat vault and dance turn by bending one leg while also playing the *lusheng*. The *Lusheng* Dance can be performed either by a group or an individual. It is common to see a male performer playing the *lusheng* for a female dancer. At the Peach Blossom Festival and other traditional festivals, fully-costumed girls and boys dance cheerfully accompanied by the *lusheng*, turning a flower field or entire village into a sea of joy.

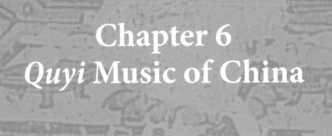

Chapter 6
Quyi Music of China

Quyi is a collective term for various narrative-singing arts of the Chinese people. It is an integrated performance art that combines music and story telling. As an art form, it has one of the longest and most distinguished histories in Chinese culture. It stresses the use of spoken language, attractive content, and tunes that are repeatable and suitable for narrating. *Quyi* also incorporates the use of facial expressions, movements and dancing, all in the service of narrative singing.

A clay figurine of a singer from the Eastern Han Dynasty.

The origin of ancient *quyi* of China can be traced back to the reciting of songs called *chengxiang* in the Warring States Period, the humorous performance of *paiyou* actors in the pre-Qin period and the responsive songs of the Han and Wei dynasties. By the Tang Dynasty, *su jiang*, a form of telling folk tales and Buddhist stories to the public appeared. *Daqu* and folk tunes also became popular, which helped narrative and singing arts to flourish. As a result, *quyi* gradually came into being as an independent art form. In the Song Dynasty, because of the development of a commodity-based economy, the prosperity of cities and the growth of the citizen class, narrative performances began to have special venues, and professional narrative artists also appeared. *Guzici, zhugongdiao, changzhuan* and other singing performances became extremely popular; about which

> **Chengxiang**
>
> *Chengxiang* is a folk narrative-singing form from the pre-Qin period. "*Xiang*" is a kind of rhythm instrument, and there are two theories regarding its origin. Lu Wenchao of the Qing Dynasty said, in a book titled *Xunzi Jiaoyu*, "*Xiang* is a kind of musical instrument, called *chongdu*." *Chongdu* originated from a tool for hulling or road construction, and later developed into a musical instrument. In another interpretation, "*Xiang*" is *bofu*. Ying Shao of the Han Dynasty said in "*Fengsu Tongyi*" (Customs): "*Xiang*, is *fu*, used in musical accompaniment. When playing music, hit the *xiang* first." According to the recordings of Liu Xi of the Han Dynasty in his book *Definitions: Definitions of Musical Instruments*, the shape of the *bofu* is like a drum. It is a musical instrument patted with the hand.

Paiyou of Pre-Qin Period
Artists with wit as their profession started their activities first among the ordinary people Later they came into royal palaces, and were called "*paiyou*" by their contemporaries. They also had singing and dancing skills. "*Pai*" itself has the meaning of "humor," and "*you*" in ancient Chinese is the collective name of all artists. In the pre-Qin period, the *paiyou* were very active, as written in the book *Shiji Humor Anecdotes* by the great historian Sima Qian, recording the activities of some *you* people such as You Meng, You Zhan, and Guo Sheren.

Xianghe Songs
The earliest record can be found in a book written by Shen Kuo in the Song Dynasty: "Respond to the *sizhu*, and the one who carries the rhythm bamboo will sing." Its feature is that the singer pats the rhythm drum and the accompanying orchestral instruments respond to the beat, from which it derived its name. Three kinds of tunes were used in *Xianghe* Songs - Sediao, Qingdiao, and Pingdiao, the same as the "Three Qingshang Tunes" of the later generations, simply referred to as "Three Tunes."

Dongjing Menghualu written by Meng Yuanlao and *Ducheng Jisheng* give detailed descriptions.

From the Ming and Qing periods to the Republic of China period, the number of cities increased dramatically, which promoted the development of narrative singing. On the one hand, folk narrative-singing with a local flavor flowed into the cities, such as the arts of *daoqing, lianhualuo, fengyang huagu* and *bawangbian*. On the other hand, some older art forms varied by combining local and dialectical features, such as the *cihua* in the Yuan and Ming dynasties gradually evolving into *tanci* in the south and *guci* in the north. In this period, new *quyi* varieties and pieces kept emerging. Most of the *quyi* varieties we see today in China are varieties passed down from the Qing Dynasty to the beginning of the Republic of China period.

After the establishment of the People's Republic of China in 1949, more than 400 *quyi* types were actively practiced throughout China. The *quyi* types of the Han Chinese can be roughly classified into five types: *pingshu, xiangsheng, kuaiban, guqu* and *zouchang*. Narrating are *xiangsheng* and *pingshu*; singing are *guqu*, such as Jingyun *dagu*, Danxian *paiziqu*, Jiaodong *dagu* and Hubei *dagu*; similar to narrating and singing are Shandong *kuaishu, kuaibanshu* and so on; narrating without accompaniment but singing with accompaniment are the *qinshu* varieties, such as Shandong *qinshu*, Guizhou *qinshu*, Yunnan *yangqin* and so forth; and walking-singing that combines narrating, singing and dancing such as *errenzhuan* (song-and-dance duet), are Shibuxian Lianhualuo and Fengyang Huagu. One actor plays multiple roles; this *quyi* artist needs no make-up, but imitates a variety of roles through narrating and singing, he or she tells all kinds of stories through performance. This form of performance is simple and direct, and its content is succinct and compelling.

Singing Tunes with Storytelling

Guqu (drum tunes) come in many different forms such as *tanci*, *dagu*, *yugu*, *qinshu* and *zaqu*. Prominent examples of these forms include Jingyun *dagu*, Xihe *dagu*, Suzhou *tanci*, Sichuan *qingyin* and Shandong *qinshu*. Of these, Jingyun *dagu* is the most popular form of *guqu* in the north of China, while Suzhou *tanci* is the most popular form in the south of China.

Jingyun *dagu* is a northern form of *guqu* popular in Beijing, Tianjin, northern China and northeast China. Its predecessor was the Muban *dagu* popular in the Hebei region. In addition to Muban *dagu*, it combines elements from *qinyin zidishu*, Beijing Opera, *bangzi* and other narrative-singing arts. In 1900, Liu Baoquan established a new performance style of Jingyun *dagu* in Beijing using Mandarin, absorbing stylish ditties and the tunes and accents of Beijing Opera, and adding an accompanying instrument, the *sihu*. Later, with the help of famous artists such as Bai Yunpeng and Zhang Xiaoxuan, Jingyun *dagu* gradually became more and more popular in northern China, establishing itself as one of the most influential forms of *guqu*.

The music of Jingyun *dagu* contains a rich variety of *banqiang* (tunes), beautiful melodies, a distinctive rhythm and is also very expressive. It is characterized by significant interval jumps and uses multiple decorative sounds to enhance the melodies. The basic pattern of the lyrics is a seven-character sentence, and each song contains around 140 to 150 sentences. Basic tunes include *manban* (slow tunes) and *jinban* (quick tunes). It is a mixture of singing and narrating, so the *yunbai*

Jingyun Drum Song has a strong expressive force.

(narrating, including the *yunbai* with *banyan* rhythm and *yunbai* without *banyan* rhythm) and singing are equally important.

The performing style of Jingyun *dagu* features one man standing and one singing. The actor controls the rhythm by hitting the *guban* (drum-board). Three people typically perform the musical accompaniment and the musical instruments used are the *dashanxian*, *sihu* and *pipa*. These are sometimes accompanied by the *dihu*. In terms of schools, Jingyun *dagu* has three major genres—"Liu," "Bai" and "Zhang"—named after its three most important exponents: Liu Baoquan, Bai Yunpeng and Zhang Xiaoxuan. Among these three masters, Liu Baoquan,

Luo Yusheng, a famous Chinese artist, presents a story-telling performance.

the so-called "King of Jingyun *dagu*," has made the most significant contributions to the development and performance of Jingyun *dagu*. Liu Baoquan was good at singing the "Three-kingdom" stories, such as *Changban Po*, *Zhaoyun Blocks the River* and *Borrowing Arrows with Grass Boats*. Bai Yunpeng was good at singing *A Dream of Red Mansions* stories, such as *Memorizing Qingwen*, *Daiyu Feels Sad in Fall* and *Baoyu's Wedding*.

Another important figure in the history of Jingyun *dagu* is Xiao Caiwu. Using the "Liu School" as her foundation, she integrated the strengths of the "Bai School" and "Young Bai School" to create the "Luo School." Her sweet voice and broad vocal range, especially her natural vibrato, created a form of Jingyun *dagu* that was much loved by audiences. She was especially good at singing the strong and loud "Ga Tones." As a result of this she became known as the "Golden Throat Singer." The classic pieces of Jingyun *dagu* not only have singing with stories, but

Pingtan of Suzhou is melodious and euphonious.

also picturesque passages used purely for expressing feelings, such as *Chou Mo Ying Chu* and *Bai Shan Tu* (Picture of a Hundred Mountains).

Tanci (storytelling) is the main form of *guqu* in southern China. It is popular in the lower reaches of the Yangtze River region, in places like Jiangsu, Zhejiang and Shanghai. Suzhou *tanci* is the most famous and popular form of *tanci*. It originated from the Suzhou region as a combination of Suzhou *pingtan* and Suzhou *pinghua*. The main performing style of Suzhou *tanci* features either a single performer or two performers, with the *pipa* and *sanxian* as accompanying instruments. The music of Suzhou *tanci* is refined and is accompanied by stories that describe the beautiful scenery to the south of the Yangtze River and love stories between intellectuals and beauties.

In the period when Emperor Kangxi ruled (1661–1722), the economy of Suzhou was prosperous. This provided an excellent environment for the development of new art forms, one of which was Suzhou *tanci*. When it came to the Jiaqing (1796–1820) and Daoguang (1821–1850) period, four former famous masters—Chen Yuqian, Yao Yuzhuang, Yu Xiushan, Lu Shizhen—and four later famous masters—Ma Rufei, Yao Sizhang, Zhao Xiangzhou, Wang Shiquan—emerged, forming the tunes of *chendiao*, *yudiao* and *madiao*, which later also became the foundation of the singing music of Suzhou *tanci*. At the end of the Qing Dynasty and the beginning of the Republic of China period, with the rise of Shanghai as a prosperous commercial center, Shanghai became another place where Suzhou *tanci* spread. Hence famous artists kept emerging from Suzhou and Shanghai, establishing multiple genres.

Singing while Walking

Zouchang means "singing while walking." Here "walking" means dancing as the music story progresses. Important examples include *Er Ren Zhuan* from the northeast and *Er Ren Tai* and *Yunan Huagu Deng* from the northwest.

Er Ren Zhuan (two-person show) is popular in Liaoning, Jilin, Heilongjiang and the eastern part of Inner Mongolia. A man and a woman act as a clown and heroine respectively. When singing, one plays with a fan and the other with a handkerchief, playing while dancing and singing. According to records, *Er Ren Zhuan* originated from the "*Zhuang Jia Shua*" (crop play) where farmers sang and danced in the flat fields. The name "*Er Ren Zhuan*" was first documented in 1934. With its basis in the northeast grand Yangge dance, it absorbed the musical elements of Lianhualuo of Hebei, and over time added new elements such as dance, posture and walking around the venue.

The song-and-dance duet, or er *ren zhuan*, is a form of folk art prevailing in the northeastern part of China.

Er Ren Zhuan has developed in all four corners of the country, resulting in a total of four genres: the eastern genre is centered around Jilin city, which has dancing with colorful rods, including the elements of martial arts; the western genre is centered around Heishan county, Liaoning province, and is significantly influenced by Hebei Lianhualuo, emphasizing Bantou; the southern genre is centered around Yingkou city, Liaoning, and follows the style of the grand Yangge, emphasizing both singing and dancing; and, finally, the northern genre is centered around Beidahuang, Heilongjiang province, and is influenced by local folk songs.

The tunes of *Er Ren Zhuan* are called "nine tunes, 18 tones, and 72 *heyheys*." Altogether there are more than 300 tunes. The *suona* and *banhu* are the main instruments of *Er Ren Zhuan*. In terms of rhythm instruments, the *zhuban* (bamboo boards, two big boards and five rhythm boards) and *yuziban* (four bamboo boards, each hand playing with two boards, also called a *"Shouyuzi"*) are used. The performance of *Er Ren Zhuan* has "four skills and one stunt." The "Four skills" are "singing, narrating, playing, dancing," and the "one stunt" refers to the use of a handkerchief, fan, *daban* or *yuziban*. Because of its smooth and lively music, witty and humorous story content, *Er Ren Zhuan* is rooted in the hearts of the northeastern Chinese people, who say, "I would rather give up a meal, than a performance of *Er Ren Zhuan*." Today, *Er Ren Zhuan* is still widely popular in the vast countryside and towns of northeast China.

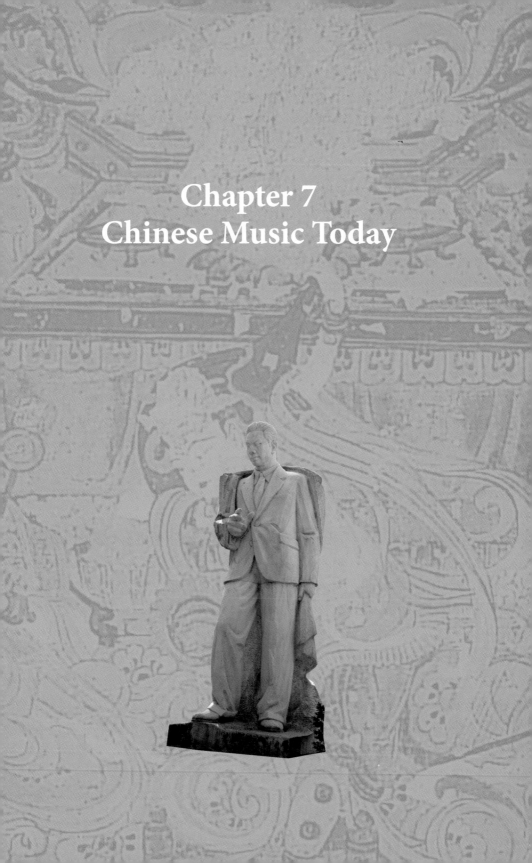

Chapter 7
Chinese Music Today

China has undergone tremendous changes during the twentieth century. There has also been increased cultural interaction between China and the rest of the world, particularly Europe and North America. Under the influence of western culture, Chinese musicians have written a new chapter in modern music by learning from and referring to western music.

Emergence of a New Music Culture

Any discussion of Chinese music in the twentieth century must start with the "School Songs." At the beginning of the twentieth century, elements of western culture began to have an influence on Chinese society. As part of this process, school music education gradually evolved with the development of new types of schools. Some foreign missionaries opened music classes in their own church-run schools. They offered a music course with rich content, called *Qin Ke*, which not only involved learning about the piano, but also vocal music, stringed music, music

Students from the department of music at Peking Women's College in 1929.

history and music composition. Some well-known intellectuals, such as Kang Youwei, Liang Qichao, Cai Yuanpei and Yang Du also introduced new theories about music education. This not only led to the beginning of music and singing courses in schools, but also to the composition of lyrics and tunes for dissemination. Some Chinese students returning from studying abroad in Japan, such as Shen Gongxin and Zeng Zhizhai, promoted singing activities in schools by offering singing classes, composing and teaching campus songs in common primary and middle schools, publishing magazines, contributing and spreading their works to some well-known domestic and international magazines, and advocating the development of new school music education. With the efforts of these pioneers, the School Songs were gradually promoted all across China.

By rescinding *keju* (the old education and talent-selection system of ancient China), promoting new schools and implementing the "Suggestions on School Music," the new education system was gradually rolled out across China. After 1912, the education administration of the Republic of China was concerned with the development of new school music education, and its main purpose was to inspire patriotism in the people—"enriching the country and enhancing military force." The School Songs of this time praised the overthrow of the monarchy, called for women's liberation and promoted equality between men and women. There were also military songs that promoted "military and public education." In terms of professional music creation in China in the twentieth century, the School Songs were the beginning.

In 1919, with the emergence of the May Fourth New Culture Movement, music societies appeared in some large coastal cities. Among these, influential new folk music communities included the China Music Society established in Shanghai in 1919 and the Datong Music Society established in Shanghai in 1929. These societies studied and performed Chinese *xiqu* and Chinese folk music, but at the same time also taught western musical instruments and theories. The Datong Music Society proposed the idea of forming a new type of folk band for the

An advertisement released by the Shanghai Electrical and Musical Industries Ltd. during the Republic of China period.

performance of ancient music and the creation of new folk music concerts. In doing so, they created *Chun Jiang Hua Yue Ye*, *Jiang Junling* and other folk music concert pieces. In 1919, Peking University established a music institute, and hired Liu Tianhua, Xiao Youmei, Chen Zhongzi, Wu Zhuosheng, Niu Lun (from the UK) and other famous musicians to provide guidance to members of the society. The president Cai Yuanpei acted directly as the head of the institute. They compiled and published fifteen issues of *Music Magazine*, which was the earliest music magazine formally published and issued in China. As a result, the creation of new types of music in China began, and various types of song quickly developed.

The development of Chinese music in the twentieth century was also influenced greatly by the return to China of a prominent group of intellectuals who had received western music education abroad. On their return, they disseminated music knowledge through music education, published books and conducted theoretical research on a new variety of music. Among them, Xiao Youmei, Wang Guangqi and Zhao Yuanren made significant contributions to music creation and music theory research.

Xiao Youmei came back to Peking from San Francisco in March 1920, teaching and composing at the Music Practice and Teaching Institute of Peking University and the Music Department of the Peking Art Professional School. In 1927, he and Cai Yuanpei and others established the first formal higher professional music institute in Shanghai—the Shanghai National Music Academy. Xiao Youmei not only made important contributions to professional music education in China in the near-modern period, but also composed many significant pieces of music and authored a number of books on music theory. His main compositions were the string quartet, *Serenade* (written in 1916 as China's first ensemble work), the piano piece *Mourning March*, the orchestral piece *New Song of Rainbow Skirts and Feather Robes* (the first piece of orchestra music written according to a western format in China), a cello piece *Thoughts in Autumn*, *Questions* and *Patriotic Song to Remember May Fourth*. Altogether he composed more than one hundred musical works. His main musicological works include *Schedule of Harmonics*, *Ordinary Music School* and *A Comparative Study of Chinese and Western Music*.

The other two important intellectuals who returned from abroad with knowledge of western music were Wang Guangqi and Zhao Yuanren. Wang Guangqi wrote a number of introductory and research works about Chinese and foreign music. His most important works are *Music Life of the Germans*, *Western Music and Opera*, *Music of Oriental Nations* and *On Classical Chinese Opera*. Zhao Yuanren was a world-renowned linguist and composer. During his career he composed more than one hundred pieces of music, which are compiled in *Collection* of *New Poetry, Collection of Songs for Children's Day* and *Collection of Public Education Songs*, among others. He combined western traditional harmonics with the Chinese national style in pieces for piano. His representative works are *Cloth Seller's Song, Song of Labor, Weaving, How Could I Not Think of Her, Going up the Mountain, Listening to the Rain, Punting on the River* and the choral work, *Tunes of Sea*, which has become an enduring part of the modern-day concert repertoire.

The Improvement of Chinese Instrumental Music

During the twentieth century, the development of instrumental music in China has undergone a series of important changes. In the first half of the twentieth century, a group of *erhu* musicians, with Liu Tianhua and Hua Yanjun as their leaders, began collecting, recording and collating folk music. Abing was also an important folk musician at this time. Absorbing and using the folk tunes in China, he created such *erhu* tunes as *The Moon Reflected on the Er-quan Spring (Er Quan Ying Yue), Listening to Pines, Cold Spring Wind Tunes*, and the *pipa* tunes *Great Tide Washes Sand Away, Zhaojun Going out of the Gate* and *Dragon Boat. Er Quan Ying Yue* is the most famous of his works as it was written after he went blind.

The tomb of Liu Tianhua, a Chinese musician, at Fragrance Hills in Beijing.

Liu Mingyuan, a famous *erhu* performer.

Liu Tianhua was a national instrumental music composer, an *erhu* and *pipa* performer, and also an important music educator. He never studied western musical instruments and learned how to perform various folk musical instruments from monks in temples. He studied and drew on the strengths of violin performance and upgraded the *erhu* from an accompanying instrument to a solo instrument. He also introduced the first professional teaching of *erhu* into higher artistic colleges, laying the foundation for contemporary *erhu* performance. He was committed to the improvement of Chinese music. He established the Chinese Music Improvement Society and became the editor-in-chief of *Music Magazine*. The *erhu* works *Moaning in Sickness* and *Song of a Bright Future* are perhaps most representative of his many compositions. They reflect his understanding of the social conditions of his time and his vision, insight and aspirations for improving national music.

Having gone through years of neglect, the *erhu* now has a very significant position in Chinese music. Through the efforts of several generations of performers and composers, the number of people who perform on the *erhu* has dramatically increased, as has the general standard of performance. From Abing's *Er Quan Ying Yue, Song of a Bright Future* by Liu Tianhua, to the more recent *River Water, Lan Huahua Ballads, Shaanxi Opera Theme Capriccio, Newlyweds Saying Goodbye* and *Great Wall Capriccio*, music for the *erhu* has experienced a renaissance in the twentieth

The Butterfly Lovers Violin Concerto
Takako Nishizaki/Violin Kenneth Jean/Conductor
The Yellow River Piano Concerto
Yin Chengzong/Piano Adrian Leaper/Conductor
Czecho-Slovak Radio Symphony Orchestra

Records of Chinese music performed by Chinese and foreign musicians.

century. This is further evidenced by recent compositions such as the *Song of the Wanderer* and *Carmen*.

It was not only the *erhu* that experienced significant developments in the twentieth century. Other national musical instruments such as the *pipa* and flute also developed in similar ways. Liu Tianhua helped to make significant reforms for the *pipa* in the 1930s, and created the Six-phase 13-grade *pipa*, which can perform traditional musical notes and twelve average notes. The Shanghai Datong Music Society also made a *pipa* in the shape of a gourd, the earliest six-phase 18-grade *pipa* in China. After the People's Republic of China was established, the *pipa* made even more progress. In the beginning the *pipa* was used only as an accompanying instrument, but today it is also used as a solo instrument. With an extensive repertoire, from pieces passed down from ancient times such as *Haiqing Hunting the Swan, Shi Mian Mai Fu*, and *High Moon* to those created in modern times such as *Dance Music of the Yi People, Five Warriors on Mountain Wolfteeth, Little Heroic Sisters on the Grassland, Weishui Qing, Spring Rain, Spring Silkworm*, there is now an impressive repertoire of works for of the *pipa*. In addition to being used as a solo instrument and part of the national orchestra, the *pipa* is also the main instrument for Jiangnan Sizhu, Canton music, Chaozhou Xianshi, and Fujian Nanyin. The *pipa* is also an indispensable accompanying instrument in southern Xiqu, Suzhou Pingtan, Sichuan Qingyin.

At the beginning of the twentieth century, the Chinese gradually accepted western musical instruments and learned the performance and composition techniques of western instrumental music. To begin with, composers simply imitated western styles. However, in time, they gave up simplistic imitation and began to develop a new style that used elements of both traditional Chinese music and western music. As early as 1934, the Russian composer Alexander Tcherepnin, or Qi Erpin, held a contest in "collecting Chinese-style piano works." *Corydon Piccolo* by He Luting won the competition. It is a piece with many typical Chinese characteristics and is still very popular today.

In 1959, He Zhanhao and Chen Gang, two students at the Shanghai Conservatory of Music, composed the violin concerto *Butterfly Lovers* (*Liang Zhu*). This now classic symphonic work has become a symbol of modern Chinese musical culture. It tells the story of a young couple named Liang Shangbo and Zhu Yingtai. The piece uses the tunes of Yue Opera (or Shaoxing Opera) and is written in the form of a concerto, combining Chinese and western styles. In terms of musical structure, the composers use the western style sonata to reflect the dramatic conflicts and also elements of Chinese folk music and opera. For example, in the presentation part it employs opera-style "dialogue" to express the theme of the love between Liang and Zhu; and, in the roll-out section, "wailing soul jumping into the tomb," it uses the *daoban* of Beijing Opera and the *xiaoban* of Shaoxing Opera. The *Butterfly Lovers* is a much-loved piece of music not only in China, but throughout the world.

Advances in technology have led to many improvements in Chinese folk music instruments, including the reform of tone and the expansion of diapason. These reforms have played an important role in the development of the Chinese national symphony. The spread and development of electronic music has also encouraged musicians to create "new folk music," which is a fascinating blend of folk music, electronic music and pop music. The "Twelve Girls Band," established in 2001, provide an excellent example

Bamboo flutist Zhang Weiliang.

of how traditional Chinese music can be successfully combined with modern musical genres. The group consists of twelve young women who all play traditional Chinese instruments like the *guzheng, yangqin, erhu, pipa, xiao* and bamboo flute. Although there is still much debate concerning the artistic value of such music, the new folk music has created a way for the popularization and internationalization of traditional Chinese folk music.

The Birth of New Opera

After the May Fourth New Culture Movement, European opera was introduced to China. The introduction of this important western art form had a strong influence on Chinese composers. The children's operas created by Li Jinhui called *The Sparrow and the Child* and *The Little Painter* enabled early school music education in China to grow from a single form of singing, to a phase of co-existence of multiple art forms. He transplanted the form of western children's musicals by nationalizing and popularizing, serving as an important reference for later music creation and opera in China.

In the 1930s, opera in China was largely based on the *xiqu* form of opera that had been around since the Song and Yuan dynasties and elements of the newly introduced European opera. This was the "new opera," a fusion of western and Chinese operatic traditions. A number of excellent "new opera" works appeared at this time, such as *Tide Tunes* (composed by Ren Guang), *Rural Tunes* (by Xiang Yu), *Zheng Chenggong* (composed by Zheng Zhisheng), *Jingke* (by Chen Tianhe), *Song of Shanghai* (composed by Zhang Hao), *Song of the Earth* (by Qian Renkang), and *Meng-Jiang Nü* (composed by Mark and Zhang Lu). The music of these operas successfully combines features of western opera with the national folk music of China.

Artists perform a *Yangge* opera—*A Brother and a Sister Open up the Wasteland*—for local people in Yan'an, Shaanxi Province..

In the 1940s, composers created operas such as *The White-haired Girl*, *Chiye River*, and *Liu Hulan*, all of which were based on Yangge Opera. Yangge is a kind of folk singing and dancing with a long history in the vast countryside of northern China. In 1943, the spectacular "New Yangge" performances held in Yan An with the Luxun Art College as the main organizer, transformed Yangge into a new form that reflected life in the frontier area. This was welcomed by the masses and was also looked upon favorably by central leaders. With the staging of the first New Yangge opera, *Pioneering Brother and Sister*, and several others such as *A Red Flower* and *Couple Improving Literacy*, the whole nation was taken over by a wave of composing and performing the New Yangge Opera.

Most Yangge Opera combined the singing and dancing of old Yangge, which included elements of local folk songs, *xiqu* and folk dancing. Such operas were designed to reflect the struggles faced in the liberated areas and the life of the army and the people at that time. In 1945, the first opera of the New Yangge

Xian Xinghai instructs students at the Yan'an Luxun Art Institute while performing the *Yellow River Cantata*.

Movement, *The White-haired Girl*, opened up a new road for the development of Chinese opera. *The White-haired Girl* was composed by the Yan An Luxun Art Institute. Its music adopted the tunes of folk songs and *xiqu* in Hebei, Shanxi and Shaanxi. The play features impressive characters like Xi'er and Yang Bailao, and famous songs such as *North Wind Blowing* and *Binding Red Hair Band*, which became popular among the people. Because *The White-haired Girl* made great achievements in terms of ideology and art, it became the opera with the greatest influence at that time. It was performed in Yan An more than thirty times and each time the venue was packed. A newspaper report of the time described one performance thus: "At each wonderful point, the applause is thunderous and lasting; at each sorrowful point, the audience sobbed, some people's eyes have tears from scene one to six...after the show, there was no one person who did not praise it."

After the People's Republic of China was founded, with the establishment of professional troupes and performances staged in theaters, a series of revolutionary operas appeared, many of which are still performed today, such as *The Marriage of Xiao Erhei, Liu Hulan, Song of the Prairie, Honghu Lake Brigade, Liu Sanjie* and *Sister Jiangjie*. The ten years of the Cultural Revolution (1966–76) brought opera creation to a standstill. However, with the reform and opening up of the 1980s, opera composition in China was again able to progress. The classic works of the 1980s are *Sad about the Past* and *Prairie*, and in the 1990s, *Marco Polo, King Chu Bawang* and *Vast Prairie*. In recent years, because of the increasing popularity of western musicals, many Chinese artists have tried to create their own musicals with Chinese characteristics. *Golden Sand (Jinsha)* and *Snow Wolf Lake (Xue Lang Hu)* are two of the most impressive Chinese musicals to have been created in recent years.

From Mass Songs to Pop Music

"Writing is for carrying the way; poems are for expressing your vision, music for voicing your thoughts." In the 1930s, with the beginning of the Anti-Japanese War, many musicians in China redirected the purpose of composition to inspire national spirit. The most outstanding representatives among these composers were Xian Xinghai and Nie Er.

After coming back to China from France in 1935, Xian Xinghai saw the sufferings of the Chinese under the oppression of Japanese imperialism. As a consequence, he actively participated in the anti-Japanese movement and composed a number of mass songs and music for

A statue of Nie Er, a great Chinese composer, in Xishan Mountain, Kunming, Yunnan Province. Nie Er composed numerous songs that presented a strong spirit of the age and distinct Chinese style. His masterpieces included *March of the Volunteers* and *A Song for Dockers*.

progressive films like *Zhi Zhi Ling Yun* (*Vision and Ambition*), *March of the Youth*, the drama *Resurrection* and *Great Storm*. In 1938, suffering extreme difficulty and hardship in Yan An, he still manage to create the masterpieces *Yellow River Cantata* and *Chorus of Production* alongside many other fine works.

Yellow River Cantata describes the dramatic changes faced by the people living along the Yellow River before and after the Anti-Japanese War. It criticizes the cruelty of the enemy and describes the oppression that the people suffered. It paints a magnificent picture of an oppressed population protecting their country and

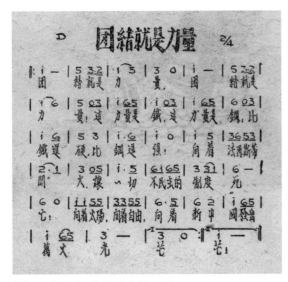

Lyrics and notation for *Unity is Strength*.

resisting foreign occupation. In this work, Xian Xinghai used elements of traditional folk music to express the revolutionary spirit of the Chinese people. As a result the *Yellow River Cantata* has become one of the most popular choral works in the history of modern Chinese music.

Nie Er was a contemporary of Xian Xinghai and, although born into a poor family, his enthusiasm for music enabled him to become a composer. However, he never forgot the hardships of his upbringing and included them in such popular songs as *Wide Road Song*, *Song of the Dockers*, *Pioneers*, *New Female*, *Graduation Song*, *Song of Newspaper Selling* and *Female Singer under the Iron Heel*. Nie Er argued that "Music is like other arts such as poems, novels and dramas; it cries out for the public, and the public surely will require new musical content and performance, and require new outlooks from composers." This view became very influential and later led to the establishment of a group of progressive musicians.

In 1949, after the People's Republic of China was founded, the country made significant achievements in terms of music education and building professional music societies. Songs for the masses also became popular. In the 1950s and 1960s, songs like *The East Is Red* and *The Long March*, and operas like *Red Guards on Honghu Lake*,

Sister Jiangjie and *Hongxia*, made a significant impact on the masses. In this period, the compositions were mainly "revolutionary" marches and new folk songs, but the marches gradually

Classic Opera *Red Guards on Honghu Lake*.

evolved to become more lyrical. All forms of music, including chorus, singing in unison, solo, ensemble and performance singing, experienced significant changes at this time.

With economic reform and opening up from 1978, some pop songs from Hong Kong and Taiwan began to enter the Chinese mainland. The songs of Teresa Teng, including *Story of Little Town* (*Xiao Cheng Gu Shi*), *Sweetness* (*Tian Mi Mi*) and *I only Care about You* (*Wo Zhi Zai Hu Ni*), were widely spread on the mainland. These pop songs from Hong Kong and Taiwan gave a new vitality to the songs of China. A large group of singers, with Li Guyi as the leading representative, began to sing in a pop style. This was the first step toward the development of pop music on the Chinese mainland. During this time, a lot of lyrical songs with national styles were made. They were highly optimistic songs that expressed the love of people towards their country and lives. Songs like *On The Hopeful Field* (*Zai Xi Wang de Tian Ye Shang*), *There the Peach Blossom are in Full Bloom* (*Zai Na Tao Hua Sheng Kai de Di Fang*), *I love you—China* (*Wo Ai Ni, Zhong Guo*), *Unforgettable Tonight* (*Nan Wang Jin Xiao*) and *Full Moon* (*Shi Wu de Yue Liang*) won great popularity among the Chinese people at this time.

Teresa Teng has had a great influence on the modern music of China.

One particular event signaled the arrival of pop music on the Chinese mainland. In 1986, more than one hundred singing stars participated in a concert in China under the title of "Let the World be Filled with Love," which was organized for the International Year of Peace. The concert was a great success. In the same year, Cui Jian, a Chinese rock singer, sang the song *I Have Nothing*, announcing the birth of Chinese rock music. Later, *Xi Bei Feng* music (a kind of pop music based on folk songs from northwestern China) became popular and Chinese pop music was gradually accepted by the whole of Chinese society.

In the 1990s, the boom of the market economy led to the fast development of Chinese music and provided further opportunities for the commercialization of Chinese pop music. Pop songs became very popular across the country, particularly those sung by famous Hong Kong pop singers such as Jacky Cheung, Andy Lau, Leon and Aaron Kwok. By absorbing the best elements of foreign pop music and the pop music of Hong Kong and Taiwan, music on the Chinese mainland developed further. A large number of pop songs were created at this time, such as *Dedication to Love* (*Ai de Feng Xian*), *My Deskmate* (*Tong Zhuo de Ni*), *So Big Tree* (*Hao Da Yi Ke Shu*) and *A Good Person will be Peaceful all His Life* (*Hao Ren Yi Sheng Ping An*). Meanwhile, other pop songs attempted to incorporate national Chinese characteristics, such as *Enter the New Age* (*Zou Jin Xin Shi Dai*), *Story of Spring* (*Chun Tian de Gushi*), *Qinghai-Tibet Plateau* (*Qing Zang Gao Yuan*), and *Way to the Paradise* (*Tian Lu*).

Cui Jian is called the "Godfather" of China's rock music.

Chinese pop music has become increasingly heterogeneous in the twenty-first century. Hip-Hop, R&B, Jazz, Rock and Chinese folk music, no matter where they come from, all have their fair share of fans. With the development of the internet and the adoption of new techniques for collecting songs, many different forms of music are now easily available for Chinese musicians and composers to draw on. Pop music is now created not only by integrating with Chinese music, but also by absorbing different elements from other forms of music around the world. It is a process of probing, discovering and forming of unique styles. Young singers and composers, such as Jay Chou, have had a profound influence on the contemporary Chinese music scene. Nowadays, Chinese pop music has won recognition all over the world.

New Music in a New Age

Since the 1980s, thanks to more and more exchanges between China and other countries, many concert performers, composers

Tang Dun has created a series of world famous musical works with traditional Chinese culture as the inspiration.

and bands visit China to give lectures, exchange opinions and perform. In the twentieth century, the works and theories of western music were introduced to China via different channels. Tan Dun, Guo Wenjing, Ye Xiaogang and some other students at the Central Conservatory of Music made important innovations in music composition. Influenced by the works, techniques and concepts of modern western music, they created an innovative body of work, including *Li Sao*, the *String Quartet No.1—Feng, Ya and Song*, and *The Poem of China* (*Zhong Guo Zhi Shi*) by Ye Xiaogang, *Mountain Songs* (*Shan Ge*) by Qu Xiaosong and the *Violin Concerto No. 1* (*Di Yi Xiao Ti Qin Xie Zou Qu*) by Xu Yashu, all of which won various prizes. This was christened the "new music."

In 1984, the first "New Music Concert" was held in Beijing. The songs played included the *Chui Da* and *Xian Shi* by Chen Yi, *Sweet Dream in the Garden* (*You Yuan Jing Meng*) and *Fu, Fu and*

Fu by Tan Dun, *The Light of the Cosmos (Yu Zhou Zhi Guang)* and *Guang Ling San* by Zhou Long, the *Long Dong* by Qu Xiaosong, *Chuan Ya Xuan Zang* by Guo Wenjing and *The Moon over the West River (Xi Jiang Yue)* by Ye Xiaogang. These songs showcased a musical style featuring vitality, creativity and novelty. In 1985, a concert under the theme of "Exploration and Pursuit" was held, with a collection of new works by young Chinese

Composer Guo Wenjing.

composers. Later, the "Tan Dun Traditional Music Concert" also attracted the attention of many people. The composer Tan Dun's music had a significant influence on the development of Chinese professional music in the middle and later 1980s and helped to create new audiences for the performance of traditional music.

In December 1985, the "Exchanging Meeting for New Works of Young Composers" was held at Wuhan Conservatory of Music. More than 130 musicians from 16 provinces and cities of China attended the meeting and performed the works of influential young musicians. During this period, many composers held their own concerts. Many of their works had significant social influence. It was not only young composers who flourished at this time. More senior composers were also able to benefit from and make contributions to the new music movement: Zhu Jian'er, with *Na Xi Yi Qi, The 6th Symphony* and *The 8th Symphony*, Luo

Zhongrong with *Picking Lotus in the River* (*She Jiang Cai Fu Rong*) and *Hidden Fragrance* (*An Xiang*), Wang Xiling, with *The 3rd Symphony and the 4th Symphony*, Jin Xiang, with *Jinling Sacrifice* (*Jinling Ji*) and the opera *Weald* (*Yuan Ye*), and Gao Weijie with the *Dream* (*Meng*) series and the *Shao* series.

From the late 1980s to the present, more and more singers and composers have had the chance to leave China and see the rest of the world. As a result, the music of modern China has become increasingly internationalized and the international profile of Chinese composers has risen accordingly. Meanwhile, a new way back to traditional music has been explored through the development of the "new music." The creation of "new music" features: 1) the application of techniques for composing western modern music in the twentieth century; 2) the integration of modern music and traditional music, absorbing elements from folk songs, folk instruments, folk dance, operas, musical story-telling; and, 3) the development of "modern folk music" and improving the performance skills of folk musicians. The "new music" is best represented by Tan Dun's *Northwest Suites* (*Xi Bei Zu Qu*) and *Nan Xiang Zi*, Guo Wenjing's *Melodies of Western Yunnan Suite for Chinese Traditional Orchestra* (*Dian Xi Tu Feng Er Shou*) and *Chou Kong Shan*, Chen Qigang's *San Xiao*, Zhu Jian'er's *Hidden Fragrance* and Zhou Long's *Flowing Water from Still Valley* (*Kong Gu Liu Shui*).

These are great times for Chinese music, with many excellent composers such as Liang Lei, Zhang Dalong, Yang Liqing, He Xuntian and Chen Yonghua and Huang Anlun. All of these composers, no matter how old they are, insist on using modern techniques to create Chinese "new music." In the twentieth century, China experienced many difficulties but eventually found the way to reform. In the twenty-first century, China's "new music" may also face challenges, but will continue to mature through the integration of foreign and traditional Chinese music.

Chapter 8
The Exchange of Music

In its long history, China has made many contributions to world musical culture. It has also integrated a great deal of foreign music. This exchange of music has lasted for more than 2,000 years. This exchange has been beneficial for both sides: foreign music has added new concepts and compositional techniques to Chinese music, while Chinese music has done much to enhance the musical cultures of other countries.

Starting with the Pitch Pipe

The exchange of musical ideas and techniques between Chinese people and foreign nations in ancient times was recorded in *Lü's Spring and Autumn Annuals: Ancient Music*. In it, the Yellow Emperor gives the musician Ling Lun the task of creating the twelve-tone system of equal temperament. That is, twelve tones that are sounded from twelve pitch pipes made of bamboo. According to this account, Ling Lun walked westwards from a place called Daxia to the northern slope of the Kunlun Mountain where he found bamboo in a stream. Today, academics have different opinions on where Ling Lun found the bamboo. Some of them argue that Ling Lun reached an ancient country west of the Congling Mountain, today part of northern Afghanistan. Others argue that he found the bamboo in the southeastern part of Gansu Province, China. Regardless of which of these is correct, the book contains fascinating details of early music in China. It shows that the economically and culturally advanced central plains became a center of Chinese music culture as early as 4,000 years ago. There can be no doubt that the tribes in the central plains had frequent exchanges with peripheral tribes, some of which were most likely musical in nature.

In 200 BC, at the time of the Western Han Dynasty, Zhang Qian was sent on two diplomatic missions to the Western Regions. In his first mission, China established direct contact with

The Silk Road
The Silk Road refers to the overland channel that was first opened up by Zhang Qian during his journey to the Western Regions. It spans over Gansu Province, the Xinjiang Uygur Autonomous Region, Central Asia and Western Asia and leads to Mediterranean countries. The road originally started in Chang'an (present-day Xi'an) in the Western Han Dynasty (202 BC–AD 138). In the Eastern Han Dynasty, the starting point of the road extended to Luoyang, Henan Province. It was given this name because silk was transported westward along this road. Its basic direction was shaped during the Han Dynasty. The road was divided into three routes: the South Route, the Central Route and the North Route. Spanning over the Eurasian continent, the trade route improved communication between China and countries in Europe, Asia and Africa.

civilizations in the regions west of China. Thereafter, countries in central and western Asia introduced their musical instruments, songs and dances to the central plains through the Silk Road, adding new color to Chinese music. In 400 AD, during the Southern Dynasty, Buddhist music was introduced from Tianzhu (present-day India) into China. Monks sang songs to attract audiences and spread Buddhist doctrines. Chinese monks translated these Sanskrit songs into Chinese.

Since the Northern Wei Dynasty (386–534), *guizi* music has had an important part to play in the cultural lives of people living in the western regions and central plains of China. This music was crucial in the development of the imperial court music of the Sui and Tang dynasties. During the three centuries of the Sui and Tang dynasties, the exchange of music reached an all-time high. The overland Silk Road spanned over countries in the western regions and led all the way to continental Europe. Through it, Christianity was introduced to China from Europe, and so were Christian hymns. At the same time, the Maritime Silk Road linked China with its neighbors Japan and Korea. In the Sui and Tang dynasties, Anguo music, Tianzhu music, Corean music (from present-day Korea) and Funan music (from present-day Cambodia) were all incorporated into imperial court music. Evidence of this influx of foreign music can be heard in such pieces as *Seven Kinds of Music*, *Nine Kinds of Music* and *Ten Kinds of Music*. These pieces all became popular song and dance works of society at the time.

The *Song of Rainbow Skirts and Feather Robes* composed by the Emperor Xuanzong of the Tang Dynasty shows the introduction and influence of Indian music in China. It is recorded that the Emperor Xuanzong was inspired to compose the *Song of Rainbow*

Grotto No 296 of the Mogao Grottoes in Dunhuang shows a scene where merchants go back and forth along the Silk Road.

Skirts and Feather Robes when he was climbing the Sanxiang Chamber on the Nuer Mountain. At around the same time, Yang Jingshu, general of the Xiliang Prefecture, presented the Indian *Brahman Melody* to him. The Emperor discovered that the Indian melody had some tones that coincided with his composition and incorporated them into his work.

The Nestorian stele, formally known as the "Memorial of the Propagation in China of the Luminous Religion from Daqin," is proof that Christianity was introduced to China in the early Tang Dynasty. "Daqin" refers to the Roman Empire, while the "Luminous Religion" refers to the Nestorian branch of Christianity. In 800 AD, Christian hymns spread to Nestorian churches and, through these churches, were gradually introduced

The Maritime Silk Road
The Maritime Silk Road refers to sea routes between China and other regions in the world. During the reign of Emperor Wu of the Han Dynasty, Chinese silk was not only transported to countries in Central Asia, Western Asia, Africa and Europe along overland routes, but also shipped via maritime routes. As a result, scholars also called this sea route linking the eastern and western worlds the Maritime Silk Road.

into China. These hymns are an important milestone in the history of the exchange of music.

After the founding of the Qing Dynasty in 1644, an increasing number of missionaries came to China from all over the world, introducing hymns and western musical instruments. The influence of these missionaries on Chinese religion was limited, but they did have a more profound impact on its musical culture. The first record of a western keyboard stringed instrument in China can be traced back to 1601. In that year, Matteo Ricci came to Beijing for the second time and presented a western harpsichord to the emperor. The European-style harpsichord was called the Atlantic *qin*.

The School Songs of the early 1920s played a crucial role in the rejuvenation of modern Chinese music. In 1902, Shen Xin'gong held a music seminar in Tokyo where he called for new lyrics for some popular Japanese, European and American songs. In 1904, the

The continuation of the *Standard Interpretation of Tone-system*.

imperial court of the Qing Dynasty approved the Authorized School Regulation and put it into effect. From then on, many new schools offered new music and song classes. Along with the influence of the School Songs, western music was introduced and prevailed in various forms such as songs and music for organ, piano and violin. Western musical notation and theory also became popular at this time. For instance, the staff was first introduced into China during the reign of the Emperor Kangxi (1661–1722), becoming popular in the nineteenth century. In addition, books on basic western music like *Yue Dian Da Zhang* (Chapters on Music), *Outline of Music Theory* and *Harmonics* were also published in large numbers.

After the Republic of China was founded in 1912, the government made music and song classes compulsory in primary and secondary schools. Since most School Songs advocated the patriotic values of "study, progress and civilization," "making China rich and building up its military power" and "saving the nation from extinction," they quickly became fashionable. In fact, School Songs helped to lay the foundation for the collective singing of China and encouraged many people to become music educators. The early School Songs were based on Japanese, European and American songs with new lyrics added to the original melodies. In 1906, Li Shutong published *The Music Tabloid*, the first music periodical available in China. At the same time, he took the lead in composing the first multi-part and three-part chorus *Spring Outing*. After him, other Chinese composers began to write lyrics.

Chinese and western music were authentically integrated with each other after the May Fourth Movement. During the May Fourth Movement, China's cultural and ideological elite started a long-lasting debate concerning Chinese and western cultures. This debate enabled Chinese people to have a thorough grasp of the value of western musical culture. From 1920, China gradually

On June 23, 2001, the world's top three tenors of Luciano Pavarotti, Domingo and Carreras gave a performance at the Forbidden City in Beijing.

established a number of professional music educational institutions, which specialized in teaching the knowledge and skills of western music. These institutions urged China to absorb the values of western music culture.

Those who made the first contributions toward rejuvenating modern Chinese music included Xiao Youmei and Wang Guangqi. Xiao Youmei went to Japan in 1901 to take advanced studies on education and music. He went to Germany to study music theory and composition, piano performance and music conducting in 1912. He returned to China after finishing his studies. In November 1928, he, together with Cai Yuanpei, founded the Public Conservatory of Music, the first independent professional music college for higher education. He composed more than 90 songs including two large-scale choral works, a string quartet *Serenade*, a solo piano piece called *Condolence*, a work for cello *Thinking in Autumn,* and an orchestral dance work called *Song of Rainbow Skirts and Feathered Robes*. He transformed music composition in China from an era of lyric writing to the stage of professional music composition.

Wang Guangqi was the founder of ethnomusicology in China. His works, such as *The History of Music in China*, *A Study on the Eastern and Western Music Systems*, *National Music of the East*, *Chinese Classical Verses, Lyrics and Poetic Dramas: Ascending or Rising Meters* and *A Study on the Translation of Musical Notations*, taught readers the theory and practice of western music in a systematic way. These works had a tremendous influence on the development of musicology in China.

The classic opera *Macbeth* is performed at the opening ceremony of the Twelfth Beijing International Concert in 2009.

Foreign musicians in China also made contributions to music education, especially in spreading western musical culture. The Russian composer Aaron Avshalomov came to China in 1914 and began to compose works in the Chinese national style in the 1920s. Some of his works, like the opera *Guanyin* and the dance drama *Inverted Reflection of Qin in Beam Wave*, were created on the basis of popular Chinese legends, stories or traditional operas. In 1934, Alexander Tcherepnin, a Russian composer, sponsored a Chinese music competition. He Luting created a piano piece with distinctive Chinese characteristics and won first prize. The work, named *Corydon Piccolo*, is a perfect combination of Chinese and western music.

Many native artists also made efforts to absorb foreign musical culture. Among them, Zhao Yuanren held tests for Chinese-style melodies and harmonies with Chinese characteristics; Liu Tianhua broke new ground in the integration of Chinese and western music; Huang Zi was a strong advocate of national music, Ma Sicong strove to create new characteristics for national music, and Nie Er and Xian Xinghai developed new musical styles.

After the People's Republic of China was founded in 1949, Chinese musical culture stepped onto a new stage. At the very beginning of this period, the Sino-foreign exchange of music was limited to the former Soviet Union and the communist countries of Eastern Europe. This limited exchange, enforced by political ideology, restricted the growth of Chinese music.

From 1966 to 1976, China isolated itself from the outside world. The Chinese-western exchange of music was at a standstill during this decade. World music, meanwhile, entered an era of pluralism in which diversified schools of music emerged one after another.

In 1978, China began to carry out the reform and opening-up policies that saw it return to the international stage. As a result, the Sino-foreign exchange of music was able to flourish once again. On the one hand, a great number of world-famous musicians and bands came to China. On the other hand, great efforts were made by China to interact with the outside world. Many works on music theory were translated into Chinese and western music scores, records and tapes were made available to the general public. Also at this time, many Chinese students were sent to study abroad, foreign music experts were invited to give lectures, and China even hosted several international academic conferences on music. All of this helped to encourage the exchange of music and ideas between China and the rest of the world.

The Spread of Chinese Music

The imperial court music of the Sui and Tang dynasties spread to other Asian countries and has had an important influence on the music of those countries. In the early Tang Dynasty, Corea (present-day Korea) began to send students to China and continued this tradition for many years. Until the early years of the twelfth century, Korean music was divided into Tang music and Corean music. The former was introduced from China and played on the same musical instruments as Chinese music, while the latter was created by Corean musicians and performed with native musical instruments.

China and Japan, separated by a narrow channel, have a long history of cultural exchange. In about 700 AD, during the Sui and Tang dynasties, Sino-Japanese cultural exchange hit a historic high. In the Tang Dynasty, Japan frequently dispatched envoys to China to learn about Chinese culture and bring back precious musical notations and instruments. In 716 AD, Kibi Makibi, a Japanese student, came to China and stayed for eighteen years. When he returned to Japan, he took a bronze pitch pipe and ten volumes of *Selections from Music Books* to help spread Chinese music theories. In 702 AD, Japan established a music school modeled on the Chinese music institute of the Tang Dynasty.

Japanese music added many elements of Chinese music culture in the process of its development. After the imperial court music of the Tang Dynasty was introduced to Japan, it attracted attention and gradually grew into *gagaku*, a type of formal Japanese music. Today *gagaku* is deemed to be an important symbol of Japanese national music. A group of Chinese musical instruments of the Tang Dynasty that are recognized as national treasures of Japan are still kept in the Shoso-in Repository of Todaiji Temple, Nara, Japan. These

The Huaxia Chinese Chamber Ensemble has put on many performances in recent years.

treasures include the gold and silver foil inlayed *qin*, the rosewood five-string lute inlaid with carved mother-of-pearl, a crooked neck lute, a moon guitar and a *kugo*.

In the twentieth century, Mei Lanfang, a great Chinese artist of the Peking Opera, gave a number of well-received performances around the world. He was invited to perform in Japan in 1919 and 1924 and also had the chance to perform with well-known Japanese actors such as Onoe Baiko and Nakamura Jakuemon. At the same time, he spread the art of Chinese traditional opera in Japan. In 1930, Mei Lanfang was invited to visit the United States for six months. During that period, he performed such Chinese operas as *Revolt of the Fishing Folks*, *Fenhe River Bay*, *Drunken Beauty*, *Farewell My Concubine*, *Chang Er Flies to the Moon* and *The Fairy Scattering Flowers*. These performances were seen all over the United States in cities such as Seattle, Chicago, Washington, San

Francisco, Los Angeles and San Diego. Such was his fame at this time that he even met with leading American artists, including the dramatists Bella Scott and Stark Young, the actor Charlie Chaplin and the dancer Rose Denis.

Mei Lanfang, a famous Chinese artist of Peking Opera, is pictured in western dress before going abroad.

Since the reform and opening up of China, the exchange of music has continued to great effect. A large number of world-renowned musicians and bands have held performances in China, while an increasing number of foreign students have come to China to learn how to play Chinese musical instruments. Meanwhile, Chinese artists have left China to demonstrate Chinese music to the world. The Chinese national music orchestra has held a New Year's concert in the Golden Concert Hall of Vienna, Austria, for several years in a row. They not only perform Chinese national music, but also play waltzes by Johann Strauss and other Austrian-style works. The have become very popular with Austrian audiences. At the invitation of Queen Elizabeth II, the China Jiangsu Kunqu Opera Troupe performed *King Lear* in the United Kingdom.

On May 18, 2001, the United Nations Educational Scientific and Cultural Organization (UNESCO) announced the first

Li Yundi, the first Chinese pianist to win the gold prize at the International Frederick Chopin Piano Competition.

Lang Lang, a young Chinese pianist who enjoys a worldwide reputation.

Song Fei, a famous *erhu* player, performs the *Qingming Festival on the River* in Tokyo, Japan.

batch of representative works of Human Oral and Non-material Cultural Heritage, of which Chinese Kunqu Opera topped the list. In 2003, UNESCO also added the Chinese *guqin* to the Human Oral and Non-material Cultural Heritage. In 2005, UNESCO also added the *muqam* of Uygur and *long tone* of Mongolia to the third batch of masterpieces listed.

At a time when countries are more closely linked to each other than ever before, Chinese musical culture has also grown to be more global and diversified. Classical music is now extremely popular and fashionable in China. Some have even speculated that the center of the classical music world may shift in the future from Europe and North America to China.

The Silk Road of Music
In 1998, Yo-Yo Ma, a world famous American-Chinese cellist, founded a non-profit music program named "The Silk Road." Over a decade, he publicized many excellent musicians of various countries and nations. He performed together with other musicians who played eastern and western musical instruments such as *pipa*, Japanese *shakuhachi* and the Indian drum. Throughout the program, he introduced these musicians and their excellent works to western audiences.

Yo Yo Ma, the Chinese-American Cellist.

A large number of famous modern classical composers and performers come from China:

Yo-Yo Ma is an American-Chinese cellist living in the United States who has produced more than fifty albums. He has won thirteen Grammy prizes and formed the Silk Road Ensemble, which provides an excellent stage for new musicians and the performance of new musical works. Besides this, he has also devoted a large amount of his time to music education, encouraging young people to learn music and prepare for careers in music.

Lü Siqing is the first Chinese person to win the gold prize at the Paganini Pemio di Violino Competition, which is recognized as the highest prize for violin players. *The Strad*, an international authoritative music magazine, says "Lü Siqing is an outstanding Chinese violin player with rare talent. He won the favor of the audience with excellent performance skills and musical feeling rich in spirituality."

Tan Dun has been recognized as one of the "Ten Most Important Musicians in the World of Music" by the *New York*

Times. He has won an Academy Award for the Best Original Score for the film of *Crouching Tiger, Hidden Dragon*, and the Grammy's Composition Prize for the opera *Marco Polo* in 1999.

Lang Lang is a renowned international concert pianist. He is known throughout the world for his technique and flamboyant style. He is the first Chinese pianist to be engaged by the Berlin Philharmonic, the Vienna Philharmonic and the top American orchestras. He also devotes much of his time to music education and, in recognition of his work, UNICEF made him a goodwill ambassador in 2004.

Other Chinese musicians that have earned distinguished reputations in the world of classical music include Xue Wei, Li Yundi and Li Chuanyun.

Appendix:
Chronological Table of the Chinese Dynasties

The Paleolithic Period	c.1,700,000–10,000 years ago
The Neolithic Period	c. 10,000–4,000 years ago
Xia Dynasty	2070–1600 BC
Shang Dynasty	1600–1046 BC
Western Zhou Dynasty	1046–771 BC
Spring and Autumn Period	770–476 BC
Warring States Period	475–221 BC
Qin Dynasty	221–206 BC
Western Han Dynasty	206 BC–AD 25
Eastern Han Dynasty	25–220
Three Kingdoms	220–280
Western Jin Dynasty	265–317
Eastern Jin Dynasty	317–420
Northern and Southern Dynasties	420–589
Sui Dynasty	581–618
Tang Dynasty	618–907
Five Dynasties	907–960
Northern Song Dynasty	960–1127
Southern Song Dynasty	1127–1276
Yuan Dynasty	1276–1368
Ming Dynasty	1368–1644
Qing Dynasty	1644–1911
Republic of China	1912–1949
People's Republic of China	Founded in 1949